THE SOCIAL MEDIA ADVANTAGE

An Essential Handbook
for Small Business

THE SOCIAL MEDIA ADVANTAGE

An Essential Handbook for Small Business

**Holly Berkley &
Amanda Walter**

Self-Counsel Press
(a division of)
International Self-Counsel Press Ltd.
USA   Canada

Self-Counsel Press acknowledges the financial support of the Government of Canada through the Book Publishing Industry Development Program (BPIDP) for our publishing activities.

Printed in Canada.

First edition: 2013

Library and Archives Canada Cataloguing in Publication

Berkley, Holly

    The social media advantage: an essential handbook for small business / Holly Berkley and Amanda Walter.

    ISBN 978-1-77040-142-6

1. Internet marketing—Handbooks, manuals, etc. 2. Social media—Economic aspects—Handbooks, manuals, etc. 3. Online social networks—Economic aspects—Handbooks, manuals, etc. 4. Customer relations—Technological innovations—Case studies. I. Walter, Amanda II. Title.

HF5415.1265.B4738 2012   658.8'72   C2012-901789-2

Illustrations by Charlene E. Nelson

Self-Counsel Press
(a division of)
International Self-Counsel Press Ltd.

Bellingham, WA
USA

North Vancouver, BC
Canada

CONTENTS

NOTICE TO READERS

1
WHY SOCIAL MEDIA MARKETING IS ESSENTIAL FOR THE SUCCESS OF TODAY'S SMALL BUSINESS

Social media is not just a marketing tactic. It's a social phenomenon that is here to stay. It is the way consumers find new products and services as well as receive the input they need to make that final purchase decision. Whether it's trying a new restaurant or seeing the latest summer movie, consumers have always relied on personal recommendations. Social media takes these recommendations to the next level. It makes what was once between two people, public. It puts word of mouth recommendations, both good and bad, out there for the whole world to see. While the voice of social media is personal, the reach is massive. And depending on what your customers are saying about you, can literally make or break your business.

To be successful in today's world of smart phones and constant connection, even small businesses need a social media strategy. The right strategy can not only help catapult your business ahead of your competitors, but also prove critical in avoiding detrimental business decisions. Social media puts the power back into the consumer's hands. And when consumers have that much voice, businesses need to listen, and act accordingly.

The Molly Katchpole story was a perfect example of how social media can magnify one customer's complaint, and force even a billion-dollar world corporation to pay attention. This is exactly what happened when the 22-year old college-graduate posted a complaint about Bank of America regarding the new $5 per month fee for using her debit card. She turned to Change.com, a web site that allows people to use social media to post petitions and solicit signatures.

Mainstream media such as TV producers and newspaper writers turn to the social web to see what's trending and hot on the public's mind. They caught wind of Molly's story and as a result, she was interviewed on TV talk shows. In the interviews, she came off as a smart, respectable young American, who people could identify with — especially those living pay-check to pay-check that were tired of extra fees big banks were imposing on them. She became the voice of what so many Americans were already feeling. In about a month, she received more than 300,000 signatures from Bank of America customers who publicly announced they were leaving Bank of America in protest of the extra fee. In the end, Bank of America removed the extra $5 fee, a decision that costs the bank more than $3.4 billion in potential additional revenue.

So let's bring this back to you, the small business owner. If you have not yet started using social media, the time is now and this book will help you get started. If you are already using social media, this book will help you further amplify your messages and help you create a social media strategy in line with your business goals.

The Time To Get Started Is Now

We interviewed hundreds of owners of small businesses across the U.S. about their use of social media and how they plan to integrate it into their overall marketing and communication strategy. There were many similar responses:

"I don't have time."

"We don't need it."

"We just haven't gotten around to it yet."

"I don't know where to start."

Even today, with its wide-spread use, many small business owners are still claiming a lack of time, resources and understanding of social media tools, as well as intimidation by the vastness of the social media space as primary factors for not yet integrating a social media strategy into their communications efforts.

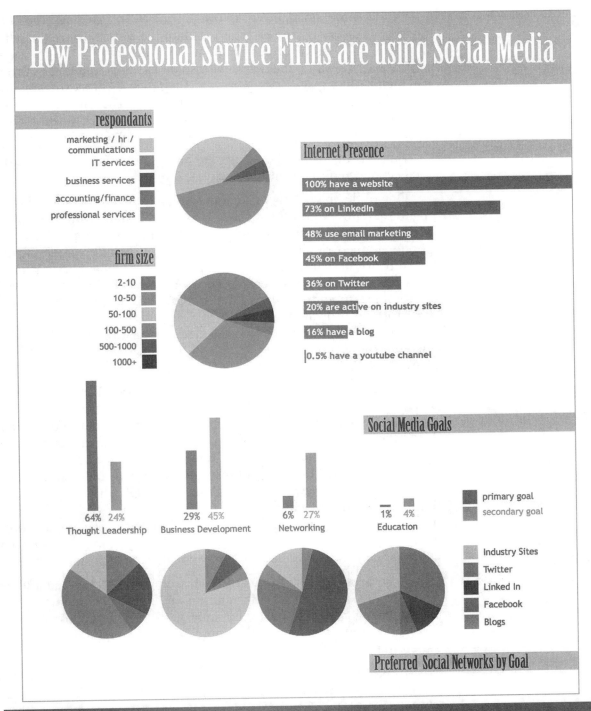

How Professional Service Firms are using Social Media

respondants

- marketing / hr / communications
- IT services
- business services
- accounting/finance
- professional services

firm size

- 2-10
- 10-50
- 50-100
- 100-500
- 500-1000
- 1000+

Internet Presence

- 100% have a website
- 73% on LinkedIn
- 48% use email marketing
- 45% on Facebook
- 36% on Twitter
- 20% are active on industry sites
- 16% have a blog
- 0.5% have a youtube channel

Social Media Goals

64%	24%	29%	45%	6%	27%	1%	4%
Thought Leadership		Business Development		Networking		Education	

- primary goal
- secondary goal

- Industry Sites
- Twitter
- Linked In
- Facebook
- Blogs

Preferred Social Networks by Goal

Figure 1.1: Results from the Social Media in Action survey conducted by ZweigWhite.

While some small business owners are still watching from the sidelines, cautiously dipping their toes into the waters of social media, there are millions of professionals who've already dived into social media and are riding that wave with some exciting results. These social media savvy professionals are watching their efforts exponentially ripple throughout the industry in powerful ways. They are successfully branding themselves as innovators in their industry by turning their social media connections into their most powerful advocates.

But like any tactic, the results are always better when they are directly connected to business objectives.

One of the major driving factors leading small businesses to investigate the effectiveness of social media as a communications or marketing platform has been the recession. "At the beginning of 2009, our phone stopped ringing," shared Laura Davis, architecture principal and director of marketing for HPD Architects in Dallas, Texas (http://www.hpdarch.com/). "It became apparent when 197 people showed up for a pre-submittal meeting that our chance for success in winning the project was dwindling. We realized we had to take action to bring in business." HPD included social media as a way to support their face-to-face networking and to expand the reach and influence of the firm's brand.

Howard Blackson, principal and director of planning for San Diego, California-based PlaceMakers (http://placemakers.com), a multidisciplinary planning and urban design firm with seven principals located in seven different cities, also points to social media as an asset for today's economic climate. He refers to social media as not only a way to conduct research and distribute thoughts and ideas, but as the core of their "New Economy" business model, which relies on the internet and social technologies to function with no overhead, no full-time office staff or central office. For PlaceMakers, social media tools allow them to run a more efficient business, bringing in expertise from all over the U.S. and Canada to easily collaborate on a single project.

Businesses of all sizes are quickly learning that social media tools enhance the efficiency of both internal and external communication needs. A single tweet or post is not only quicker than traditional forms of communication, but can reach more people faster and has a longer "shelf-life."

According to a 2011 survey (http://www.umassd.edu/cmr/studies andresearch/socialmediaadoptionsoars) from the University of Massachusetts Dartmouth Center for Market Research, more companies than ever view social media as an essential asset to business communications, with 86‰ reporting that social media technologies were "very important" to their business and marketing strategies in 2010. According to the survey, 71‰ of businesses used Facebook in 2010, 59‰ used Twitter and more than half surveyed blogged. Of this group, 85‰ view Facebook as successful in helping them meet their business goals, while a whopping 93‰ report message boards as a successful tactic.

As one social media advocate, Vik Duggal (@VikDug), said "The internet is about 17 years old, just about to graduate high school and is about to really blow up." Social media is even younger.

Although still young, social media has already become an essential piece of most business's overall communications strategy. Business owners are sharing ideas on Twitter, growing their customer base with Facebook, promoting their expertise on blogs — and seeing measurable return on investment for their efforts.

Today's social media tools aren't only about technology. They are a direct response of today's business world where communications happen in real time. Think of social media as the new cell phone. Just as each and every one of your employees and consultants has a direct cell phone number to power their everyday business and communications, social media can also be leveraged for this purpose — but contains a longer and stronger shelf-life than a single phone call. But unlike a phone call that is between a closed or private group, social media communications allow for outside input and influence, which will help your ideas and your business expand and thrive. Social media offers the ultimate "listening tool" to gain honest input from customers, feedback on your products or services and your business, as well as to discover new and more efficient ways of working.

When social media tools are leveraged in the right community setting, whether that includes employees of an organization, a group of people with a common interest or goal or a community of residents sharing the same town or neighborhood, members are compelled to interact and share their perspectives. Listening to those conversations and ensuring that you are engaging on topics that matter most to your core audience is the essential ingredient for making full use of social media as a multi-directional communications tool.

This new way of thinking is an opportunity for all businesses to reorganize their overall communication strategy, decision-making authority and how information flows out to the public, customers, your supply chain and employees. During your deep dive into social media, you will start interacting with customers and colleagues in a way you have never done before, and as a result you will start to build deeper relationships. Ideally, these deeper connections will be the online advocates who will carry your message further than you ever could have imagined on your own. After all, people prefer to buy from other people, not impersonal mission statements, statistics, websites and corporate logos. This new form of media is not a trend. It is the way businesses communicate.

Where Do I Start?

Time and intimidation were the main reasons businesses gave us for not having integrated social media into their communication strategies. Small business owners said they were so busy running their business and day to day operations that taking extra time to update a blog, find connections on LinkedIn or post a tweet was just too much. Plus, since many industries are still finding themselves on the tail end of a major recession, priorities are on selling through traditional offline methods. For many business owners, these types of traditional approaches to sales feel safer. However in this book, we'll show you how social media can open your business up to a wider group of potential customers, and provide more reach than a single hand shake and paper business card ever could.

Social media isn't a stand-alone program; it should come alongside a company's strategies and business objectives that are already in place. Once you know what you are trying to accomplish, the most important piece of advice for jumping into the social media world is this: You don't have to be everywhere. It's better to have a strong, influential voice on a handful of social networks where your target audience lives than to try to be everywhere at once. There are so many channels of information available; not only would trying to excel at each be overwhelming, but it is impossible. As shown in figure 1.2. Trying to be everything to everyone will not help you be effective in your social media use. In fact, it will achieve the opposite. It will dilute your overall influence in your online social circles. Focus your approach on a specific objective.

Getting Company "Buy-In"

Before you sign up for your first Twitter account or register a name for your blog, define what your business's overall communication goals are. Just like any marketing and communication vehicle, you have to plan for how you will use social media and how you will measure the success of your efforts.

scattered   focused

Figure 1.2: Trying to excel at each channel is impossible.

You should also recognize that there is a misconception about social media: that engagement is cheap or even free. Although the social media tools themselves are free, building solid online community profiles takes company buy-in, organization and an investment in time and resources. Your business's social media cannot be run by your high-school aged child or some random intern. What goes out on the social networks must reflect your company's intellect, quality, brand, mission and be aligned with your overall business goals. Therefore, the content and messaging needs to be managed by someone with a vested interest and passion for the company and the topic at hand. Social media, when used correctly, can effectively support the communications for most groups within your organization, from PR and marketing to research and development, and from knowledge management to internal communications and recruiting.

The First Step

Start with the end in mind. It's essential to understand your goals and objectives. These will drive the decisions around your target audience and what you are trying to get them to do.

If you do not know your goals, conduct a thorough analysis to set them. There are several widely published methodologies for goal setting, like the Strengths, Weaknesses, Opportunities and Threats (SWOT) analysis that can help you narrow your focus; or the SMART method— Specific, Measurable, Attainable, Realistic and Time sensitive—which is an acronym to help you check that your goals are result-oriented. Regardless of how you approach it, this step is essential. Before starting any communications engagement with clients — whether we are looking into social media or not — we begin with a question and answer session to get to the heart of what they want to achieve and what vehicles are best suited for their goals. See the *Objective and Strategy Setting Worksheet* sidebar for an outline of questions that drive these conversations and tips for setting objectives.

Objective and Strategy Setting Worksheet

Jumping into social media without forethought and planning is perhaps the biggest, and most common, mistake that a small business can make. Without an objective and a strategy, there is no real way to measure, test, achieve success or determine failure. We use the principles of Strengths, Weaknesses, Opportunities and Threats (SWOT) combined with the information we've come to rely on for marketing or communications campaigns to help assess the landscape and zoom in on a good approach. This fact-finding assessment can take a general, company-wide focus or it can be specific to each market sector or service offering.

Establish Objectives

What is your mission statement, values and/or brand attributes?

- What are your business goals?

- What are your marketing goals?

- What is the reputation that you aspire to have?

- What parts of your business support these goals? Examples are core competencies and differentiators.

- Who in your company is instrumental to reaching these goals in roles such as a subject matter expert or inspiring leader?

- What has the company done and/or is currently doing to advance toward these goals?

- Who are your clients? Who is the decision maker of these client firms and who are the influencers? What is this influencing-person's background? What does their job entail?

- Who are your competitors? How are they communicating? Is it effective?

- Are there sensitive issues or topics that perhaps we need to keep in mind or avoid talking about in public?

Establish a Strategy

- What does success look like?

- What assets are unique to your business? These might be research and development, image library, events, marketing programs, breakthrough projects.

- What are your resources that can be assigned to this effort? Examples are in-house staff and outsourced resources like agencies or consultants.

- Who are these resources and what is their background, areas of expertise, interests? How much time are they allowed to spend on it?

- What networks or organizations are your company and/or its leaders actively involved in? What is the nature of the involvement such as a sponsor or board member?

There is an old advertising adage that states a person needs to see a message seven to 12 times before they commit it to memory. It is important to find multiple ways of reaching your audience to make your messages stick. Social media should not be an isolated program and it should not replace your existing communications channels, rather it should integrate with them. Your social networks are simply communications channels. The content that you use on the social web should complement, pull from, and promote the pieces of your existing marketing programs, such as your newsletters, direct mail and events.

Finally, before starting a social media campaign you must be prepared for flexibility. Social media tools and rules change frequently. Although you are not expected to be a social media expert, your company must be able to make a quick decision and respond in real time to crises as well as positive PR opportunities that arise.

Proper use of social media is about decentralized decision-making where everyone in your company can contribute and have a voice. However, before letting just anyone in your organization tweet or post on your company's behalf, defining guidelines and core messaging is essential. Setting up the right internal structure and goals before you engage in the social space is key to making it work for your company.

We'll get into the internal behind-the-scenes tactics for generating ideas, recruiting contributors and empowering employees in Chapter 4.

You rely on the knowledge and success of individuals within your company as a pillar of the firm's reputation. In Chapter 5, you'll find strategies that are being used at some of the most recognizable businesses that are positioning their experts in front of their brand. We'll address the risks and benefits of this approach, how some are embracing their thought leaders, and the changes they are seeing because of it.

Social media tools continue to grow and evolve based on the needs of today's business user. The most exciting thing about social media is that unlike any other form of media, you can track the results of your effort instantly. As you engage in social media, you'll learn that a simple tweak in the way you compose a blog post headline, or the time of day you tweet can make a significant impact on the results you will see.

As you engage in the tactics outlined in this book, we'd like to hear how you are doing. Find us online at www.The-Social-Media-Advantage.com to connect with us via your favorite social network. Here you will find links to share ideas and ask questions. We look forward to hearing from you.

2
FINDING YOUR TARGET AUDIENCE / DETERMINING THE BEST SOCIAL NETWORK FOR YOUR BUSINESS

By the time you finish reading this sentence, there will be 700 new posts on Facebook. By the time you finish reading this chapter, there will be more than 1 million new tweets. With more than 1.9 billion Internet users world wide (RoyalPingdom.com, June 2010), watching millions of videos, creating millions of blogs and updating posts, status updates, and comments on a daily basis, finding your target audience in the sea of social media can feel overwhelming.

Stop. Take a deep breath. Realize that in order to be successful on the social web, you do not have to be everything to everyone—or everywhere for that matter. In fact, no one can conquer every online social network. There is simply too much information flowing every second. Therefore rather than trying to tackle every social network at once, focus on the handful of social spaces where your target audience is most active.

As you start using social media to find and communicate with different audiences, you will quickly discover that some social networks provide more immediate benefits to your overall goals than others do. You may also discover that it can take a combination of many social networks to promote your message most efficiently. Because online communications are more measurable and trackable than traditional forms of communication, the more you listen and engage on different social networks, the more you will be able to refine your efforts to maximize efficiency and attain your desired goals. (You'll learn how to track, measure and evaluate your social media efforts more in Chapter 7.)

PlaceMakers, LLC, is a small company made up of independent consultants primarily focused on the reformation of municipal zoning codes, as well as master planning and urban design for private developers. Through social media use and engagement, they have discovered that it takes a combination of social tools and messaging to reach their audiences and goals.

Scott Doyon, Atlanta, Georgia-based principal and director of marketing of PlaceMakers, LLC, (http://placemakers.com) describes effective social media outreach as a delicate balance of several tools. He advises that small business owners look at their social media profiles and fan bases as a tool box. The more you engage on the sites and understand how they work and help the lives of your audiences, the better you will understand which tool to use, and when.

On any social networking site, such as Twitter and LinkedIn you can easily search by keyword, topic, job function or company name and you'll be presented with a list of tweets, profiles, pages, groups and so on. Once you identify where your target audience is, take some time to listen.

This is a strategy that Christine Morris, communications and special projects coordinator of Construction Specialties, Inc. (http://www.c-sgroup.com), in Muncy, Pa. has found success doing. "Our target audience is made up of customers, potential customers and other influencers," explains Morris. "Our first step in deciding which networks to use was to spend some time watching, listening and researching to see where this target audience was spending their time and where they were posting* on a consistent basis. We simply met them where they are."

Think of joining a new social networking group as stepping into a cocktail party where you don't know anyone. You wouldn't start loudly announcing your business and latest offerings the second you stepped foot in the door. Not only would this be rude, but it would be a complete turn off to all the other guests. Instead, take smaller steps. See figure 2.2. Listen. Ask questions. Find out who the key influencers are in that group and get in their good graces. Also, pay attention to how the group talks, the lingo they use and how they interact with each other. You want to fit in.

Social Media Tips from Cocktail Party Etiquette

Be subtle
Listen
Ask questions
See who is most influential
Be patient
Be relevant
Be sincere
Have fun

Figure 2.2

Never directly push your business. Instead, contribute meaningful information that your target audience is seeking. Don't be afraid to give it away for free. Encourage dialogue that helps position you as a knowledgeable person in your industry and as someone who cares about others' thoughts, problems, concerns and opinions. Spend more of your time on social sites talking to people, building relationships, sharing resources that aren't your own products or services than you spend promoting yourself and your company. Through this type of engagement and understanding of the audiences, you will be more likely to capture the right kind of attention, along with trust and loyalty.

Once you are an accepted member of the group, test out new approaches and dialogues. Have fun with it. After all, social networking is still in its infancy as a field of interest and study. Best practices and tactics in the field are continuing to evolve. Many small businesses are benefiting from a combination of traditional and social marketing. While social media helps open doors to new leads, many small businesses have found that more traditional follow up tactics help them to actually close the deal. Read the side bar from TKO Graphix to learn how they used a combination of social networks and traditional sales to help them land a 2 million dollar project.

Case Study

Combining Social Media outreach with traditional sales strategies helps land $2 Million Dollar Sale from Flickr lead

Company Overview

TKO Graphix is a full-service graphics provider in Plainfield, Indiana, established in 1985. We design, manufacture, and install graphics for fleets, vehicles, retail, events, and trade shows. We also offer signage services nationally. Our customers include Target Stores, Celadon, HH Gregg, Interstate Distributing, and Knight Transportation, among others.

Marketing Goals, History

Our goal in using social media has been to better connect with our current customers, while finding new prospective customers and associates to work with. We also wish to maximize our web presence and engage our demographic through a more personalized experience.

In 2009, we launched our social media presence, and have since established accounts on Flickr, Twitter, Facebook, YouTube, Google's G+ and LinkedIn, along with our Brandwire Blog. As with all our networks, we expanded our Flickr presence daily by publishing new photographs of our work, searching for current customers and prospects (Flickr search), and searching via common keywords respective of our industry. New contacts were emailed a brief, personalized note to welcome them, which led to my (Josh Humble) connecting with a print broker in St. Louis, IL. I then introduced him to Glenn Burris, one of TKO's national account representatives. Glenn drove to St. Louis, where they talked about how we could help each other. The broker was contacted by an ad agency that needed a large format graphics company with traveling installation crews. This led to TKO presenting to a large national company. After meeting with the national company for a second time, TKO provided a proposal and was awarded the contract.

A Multi-Faceted Marketing Plan

- *Social Media:* Publishing our portfolio to Flickr, while adhering to best practices for titles, description tags.

- *Social Networking:* Proactively seeking prospects and engaging with target audience via the network.

- *Traditional Networking:* Meeting face to face with prospectives.

- *Sales Presentation:* Presenting in-person to the prospective customer.

In the middle of a very challenging recession, 2009 was our best year yet, thanks to the power of social media and engaged marketing.

We re-branded over 4,000 vehicles at 221 locations in North America for the national company. We also manufactured all decals and wraps, de-identified their vehicles, and installed new graphics, while creating an online fulfillment program for easy ordering.

Understanding and using all traditional forms of applicable marketing, in conjunction with new media marketing, has been one of our biggest lessons learned. Social media works - however, we always need to be where our audience is.

Considering our markets are composed of both traditional AND new media demographics, keeping a balance of mediums and tools used has been greatly beneficial.

—Josh Humble
INTERACTION DESIGNER, PHOTOGRAPHER, AND SOCIAL MEDIA STRATEGIST FOR *TKO GRAPHIX*

www.tkographix.com

Focus on relevant, quality messaging, not quantity, to attract your audience.

When local plumber, Tim McKenna of McKenna Plumbing canceled his newspaper and Yellow Page ads to save money, he eventually turned to Twitter to drum up business. He quickly learned that a subtle, more conversational approach won out over direct, hard selling. Although his Twitter handle @itstheplumber, identifies his profession, his bio is friendly, sharing that he "loves tango, yoga, rowing, endurance sports."

"Forget about the number of followers," said Mckenna, "It's most important to connect with the people who do follow you."

McKenna learned this first hand when a follower with a plumbing issue reached out to him on Twitter. The follower's kitchen sink lost water pressure and she was hoping to find a quick fix online. McKenna ended up resolving her issue via a phone call, however the expert advice resulted in a quality Twitter testimonial for everyone to see.

In specialized fields or niche industries especially, quality trumps quantity every time. In other words, it's better to have a few hundred Twitter users who subscribe to your tweets ("followers") who are your core audience and care about what you have to say, than to have thousands of followers that will never notice you or become your online advocates by retweeting and responding to what you have to say. The same idea holds true with blogging*. Its best to have well-crafted, thought out blog posts that convey your brand messaging while providing insightful opinions and information than to post mindless chatter every day. It's the quality posts that will get forwarded, linked to, picked up by various RSS feeds* and help your online presence grow.

Figure 2.1: Building a focused social presence and crafting quality content will generate a targeted following that is more likely to engage and help share your messages.

Understanding not only who your target audience is, but why they are engaged on a specific social network, is important. You want to understand what kind of information they are seeking in a particular social space and be able to provide that to them. For example, your Facebook friends* may want to see different types of information than those who subscribe to your blog. Through testing and tracking which types of posts and information gain the most feedback in the form of comments, likes* or shares*, you will be able to optimize each social communication channel to benefit each audience, and therefore get closer to reaching your specific business goals.

A 2011 study by Razorfish found that among all social networks, friends, followers and fans cited "feeling valued" as the most important element of engaging with a company online. Therefore it isn't just about providing your audience with the type of information they seek; "companies should worry less about building out numerous channels and touch points and more about ensuring each customer interaction communicates value," Razorfish says.

Ensuring value and quality posts is something PlaceMakers, LLC seems to weave effortlessly into their communications. The principals of PlaceMakers create well-thought-out blog posts that generate emotion and response, while they also fit powerful observations into 140 characters or less on Twitter. Creating a message that generates emotion and response is what social media is all about. After all, social media is designed to spark dialogue between individuals to create a feeling of community. It is not a successful tool for simply pushing company announcements and press releases. Those types of posts and tweets will probably not succeed in the social media space.

"We see ourselves less as individual planners, designers, marketers, etc. and more as cultivators of community," said PlaceMaker's Doyon. "Instead of just writing for other planners, we're building relationships with environmentalists, developers, city boosters, bike and pedestrian advocates and all kinds of other folks who care about community improvement."

PlaceMakers has cast a pretty wide net to cover their target audiences. But they don't do this by having one marketer or sales person doing all the tweeting, posting and chatting. Instead, PlaceMakers is able to reach many different types of audiences with valuable, thoughtful information, because they allow each team member to blog, tweet and post about subjects that are most important to them. This approach helps pave the way for each team member to begin establishing themselves as potential thought leaders in their specific areas of interest and expertise.

Deborah Reale, community manager and marketing specialist at Reed Construction Data of Norcross, Georgia (http://www.reedconstructiondata.com/), has developed a similar social media strategy for Twitter. Rather than trying to push messages out and listen to all the feedback and chatter at once, she recommends segmenting Twitter followers by area of expertise, to keep better track of feedback as well as provide useful information in a more organized and powerful way.

"I'm a doctoral candidate in business, so to me, Twitter is similar to a strengths, weaknesses, opportunities and threats (SWOT) chart," explains Reale of her Twitter strategy. "If a firm has its 'following' organized and lists them properly, management should be able to discern the SWOT for products, the organization, competitors, customers, prospects; even the industry itself."

By using social media sites like Twitter as a listening tool rather than just blasting promotional messages, Reale discovered that Twitter can help her company reach goals beyond marketing and sales and aide in customer service management as well as product creation and improvement.

"I believe that in business-to-business (B2B), people respond to people. Most companies segment by product or customer base. I thought it might be a good idea to segment by our people in their area of expertise. I wanted to put a human face on the RCD segments," said Reale.

Twitter allows users to easily segment followers and the people they follow through the creation of lists. Some organizations even develop completely different Twitter accounts for each content area of their company to allow for strategic development of different types of customer leads and distribution of more targeted information. By creating different Twitter accounts and dividing followers into specific lists, Reed Construction Data is able to have different individuals within Reed Construction Data share information that is most valuable to each target audience and therefore create more loyal followings.

How a Targeted Facebook ad Helped Orabrush get on the shelves at Walmart

We were already in contact with Walmart Corporate Offices through traditional sales channels. Their local vendor program allowed individual Walmart managers to pick up local products for local stores shelves. We'd had a manager here in Utah request Orabrush to carry for the holidays, and from that introduction, many other local Walmarts picked us up as well. Sales were robust, and the prospect for an expanded Walmart launch beyond our area seemed very good, but we wanted to speed up the process.

We made a DVD with a personalized introduction for the sales rep we'd been in contact with at Walmart HQ. When the DVD starts, The Orabrush Guy and Morgan the Orabrush Tongue (our two spokesman of YouTube fame) address the rep by name and discussed all the sales figures we'd seen in our test market in UT. We included samples of our videos, user reviews, and the press coverage we'd gotten. It was unique and thorough, and we were confident it would have their attention.

Part of our strategy was to come from as many angles as we could, through the traditional sales channels, and then with the DVD. But we're a social media company as much as we're a consumer goods company. Our world is web advertising.

I had the idea to use Facebook ads in a very targeted way. In college, I'd used Facebook to target a single girl to ask out. It was narrowed down to only girls with this name who went to this college who are from this hometown with these interests. Now I promise this isn't as creepy as it sounds; we already knew each other and it was a fun way to surprise her. Facebook won't allow that narrow of targeting anymore, probably to prevent potential creepiness like I'd done, but the technique still works, even with an audience broader than one. I suppose the girls of Provo UT (home of Orabrush HQ) can be glad I'm now happily married. No more Facebook pro stalking.

We created a Facebook ad targeted only to Walmart employees in Bentonville Arkansas who have a college degree. The only people who meet those qualification are employees at Walmart HQ. We were reaching the executives. The ad said "Walmart Employees have bad breath! Walmart needs to carry Orabrush! It will sell better than anything in your store!"

Two days and $28 in ad spend later, we got an email from a Walmart VP, letting us know that they'd seen our ad, and would we please take it down. They seem to have gotten the impression that we were broadcasting this to the country, not realizing it was targeted to their office.

They'd already heard we were good at reaching our desired audience online. Now they knew it firsthand.

—Submitted by Jeffrey Harmon,
CMO of Orabrush www.orabrush.com

Never Interrupt. Instead, Foster Dialogue.

The biggest mistake marketers make with social media, regardless of industry, is interrupting rather than contributing to the conversation. By using your own employee resources to add expertise to conversations, you can provide more authentic value to target audiences.

"My twitter feed highlights social media, marketing and business/ technology news, with a spotlight on our industries," described Reale of how each employee contributes different content to the segmented Twitter followers. "Another Reed employee, Kathy, is a technical writer for building product manufacturers. Kathy tweets a good deal about manufacturing and she follows and talks to manufacturers on her Twitter feed. She understands their pain points, the stuff that keeps them up at night." We'll talk more about how you can engage your employees in social media in Chapter 5.

For companies trying to reach several different target audience groups, segmentation allows the ability to provide specific information that is useful and relevant to the needs of each audience group. The result of this relevant information is that it can, in turn, develop stronger, deeper connections with each audience. Reale believes this type of segmentation will help Reed Construction Data develop better products by listening to feedback and asking questions to the right audiences. And Twitter is not the only social network to benefit from segmentation. We are also seeing more businesses that have set up multiple blogs, each focusing on different topics to appeal to various audiences. You can also set up lists within your Facebook profile so that specific messages will only go out to those "friends" most interested in your company updates. To set up a different list in Facebook, simply click on "Friends", then "Edit Friends." From here, you will see a link that says "Create a List." This will allow you to name the list and add certain Facebook friends to that list. Similar lists can also be set up in Google+. These lists are called Circles.

It is important to note that social networks are not just for the young. Internet users between ages 34-44 are dominating the social media space, becoming the fastest adopters of social media use. This audience represents the incoming wave of industry leaders since they will be the 50-year-olds likely running larger corporations and in charge of making major company purchasing decisions in 10 years. From our conversations with such industry folks, they understand that using social media helps them reach a variety of business goals efficiently, from positioning themselves as knowledgable, to finding new clients, to keeping a pulse on what is happening in the their industry.

While the large social networks (Facebook, LinkedIn, Twitter, YouTube, Google+) can provide great reach and access to many people, small businesses are learning that the more niche, topic-specific social networks can actually provide better access to potential clients directly seeking their services. For example, CosMed Plastic Surgery Center (www.cosmedclinic.com) frequently posts answers to community health questions in plastic surgery and weight loss online communities: MakeMeHeal.com and ObesityHelp.com. People who participate on these forums represent a core audience for the plastic surgery center and allow them to build a more personal connection with potential customers who may hesitate to share health concerns on a more public forum such as Facebook.

Social media happens fast, and new niche networks and blogs arise almost daily. A great tool to help you stay current with these websites and also monitor the pulse of the online conversation your industry is Google Alerts. This is a free tool that will email you when your chosen keywords are talked about online. Simply go to google.com/alerts and enter keyword phrases, such as your company name and hot topics related to your industry, along with your email address to be notified each time anything related to these topics appears online. As professional social media and communications consultants, Google Alerts is an invaluable tool to discover new blogs and smaller, more niche communities that are discussing hot topics where our clients would benefit from being heard.

Sometimes what looks like the smallest online community to an outsider can actually have powerful voices developing opinions and dialogue that will eventually spill over to the more trendy social networks. Understanding these core audiences, who the key influencers are, what issues are most important to them and how to get your company, products and services in their good graces can be an invaluable asset. Listening, monitoring and helping to guide dialogue on these niche, smaller sites can help you better understand the thought process behind what motivates your core audiences to support your company and your future products and services.

This listening technique can also help you avoid a major PR nightmare on sensitive projects. It allows you to see negative comments coming before the conversations gain leverage in front of major media channels on the bigger social networks.

In addition to helping you discover new places your company should engage, setting up a Google Alert with your own company name as the keyword allows you to be notified anytime anyone online is talking about your company. Being able to listen in to what audiences are saying about you and having a chance to respond is what gives social media such powerful reach. If you are simply using social media to post press releases and company announcements you are missing the point of social networking. Monitoring the online responses to these press releases and announcements is the real power of social media.

As you dive deeper into social media, you will want to use more advanced social monitoring tools. Companies like Lithium Technologies (ScoutLabs.com) and Radian 6 (http://www.radian6.com) allow you to track and engage with anyone who is mentioning your company on the social web. Using either of these website tools, simply type in your company name or a product name and see what people on Facebook, YouTube, Twitter, blogs, websites or news articles are saying about your company and products. Almost anything that is mentioned on the social web will pop up using these listening tools. These social monitoring tools go deeper than Google Alerts as you can actually click on the post from the application and respond to the online discussion in one step.

Social media monitoring tools can also be valuable at helping you monitor your competition. For example, while consulting for Verizon, we used the Scout Labs dashboard (now a part of Lithium's Social Media Monitoring) to compare online sentiment for AT&T to Verizon. Within seconds, a graph showed that Verizon has more mentions and more positive overall sentiment on the social web than AT&T.

The social web is essentially the world's biggest focus group allowing you true insight into what your customers are saying. Additionally and better than the focus group, the social web gives you the real-time ability to respond and add to this discussion. You don't have to be a major company like Verizon to generate an overwhelming amount of social comments from customers that need responses from your company. Perhaps you are just in the midst of a heated online debate about a new project, which is developing hundreds of posts you'll need to monitor. Fortunately, applications like Lithium's Social Media Monitoring not only show you every place your company name is mentioned, but conveniently sorts posts in order of priority, so you can know which posts are most important to respond to. The program determines priorities based on several critical factors, such as how much traffic the web site gets, Google rank, how many people are actively reacting/responding to the post and perhaps most importantly, the online influence of the person who made the comment.

Understanding Key Influencers Within Your Target Audience Group

Determining the identity of key influencers within your online social networking circles can be critical to your goals – especially if you tend to carry controversy around specific projects or individuals within your company. How the key influencer in a social circle regards your company can make or break your mission. When this influencer loves your company or project, you can sit back and watch the positive energy flow, but get on their bad side, and you may be confronted with a PR nightmare.

No matter the size, every online community has its loudest voices. And these voices make up only 1% of the total community. But they are a powerful 1%. This select group is essentially the "creator." They are the ones who start conversations and keep the discussions alive over the course of several days or weeks. The creators have a huge influence on the attitudes and energy of the social group.

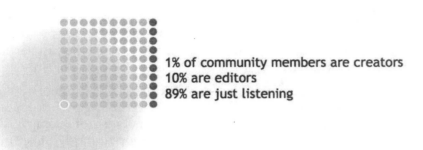

1% of community members are creators
10% are editors
89% are just listening

Figure 2.3

It may appear that a social network is not active or that no one is listening due to the small percentage of participants actually creating content. As shown in figure 2.3, 10% of a community is what is known as "editors." These members will post and contribute to conversations started by the "creators." They are the ones who will simply "like*" something on Facebook, or contribute a "me too" type blog comment.

So what are the remaining 89% of the members doing? Listening.

Even though you may think no one is paying attention to your posts and comments, they are. Social media provides a voyeuristic view of what's happening in your community. For the same reason reality television took off, social media offers a chance for people to listen in, see your ideas and hear what's going on in a fairly anonymous way.

Finding New Employees On Linkedin

LinkedIn provides an ideal way for you to find new employees, vendors and even open yourself up to new customers and projects. In today's online world, more and more people in charge of hiring look to recommendations on LinkedIn before anything else. Of our survey of business professionals, 73% are actively using LinkedIn, and more than half are using it to recruit and to connect with vendors, partners or subconsultants.

"I put a lot of weight on referrals received via Twitter and LinkedIn," admits Amy Good, vice president of finance/business manager of Lancaster County Timber Frames of Lititz, Pennsylvania. She uses LinkedIn frequently in her company's search for employees, partners or vendors.

Making sure your personal LinkedIn profile is complete, up-to-date and you have quality reviews is a great way to help your profile show up in LinkedIn's professional searches, which helps your target audiences find you.

The primary benefit of LinkedIn is the ability to connect with other people in your industry and for the opportunity to get introduced to their connections, thereby expanding your network of quality business contacts very quickly. Once your profile is up-to-date, LinkedIn will help you easily find your connections by content pulled from your profile, such as past employers and the schools you attended.

But adding a profile and connecting with others in your industry is only a minor part of LinkedIn. There is an extremely targeted, active question and answer community happening behind the scenes in the LinkedIn social network. Not engaging in these discussions is like showing up at a networking event and not talking to anyone, but just signing in at the registration table and maybe dropping a business card in the fish bowl in hopes someone might notice you and give you a call, but not attending any break-out sessions or social hours. You are a LinkedIn wallflower if you are passing up the opportunity to chime in on these discussions.

Only 20% of our survey respondents are using LinkedIn to demonstrate thought leadership or advance the intellectual brand of their company. Depending on your profession, there are likely plenty of active LinkedIn groups dedicated to your specific industry, that could use more expert voices. There is a search function at the top of your LinkedIn page where you can input keywords relevant to your work or research which professional organizations, groups or magazines the other key players in your industry belong to. Join as many as you can realistically keep up with. You'll quickly find that these resources can provide an excellent way to show off your expertise to the right potential client or partner who is looking for your skills.

Most LinkedIn groups are created with a particular audience in mind. Often, the administrators will only approve new members that fit this demographic.

Can't find an existing LinkedIn group that meets your goals? Start a new one. In Chapter 8, we'll provide tips on how to build and nurture a social media community.

Reaching Your Goals With Twitter

By 2013, nearly 28 million Americans will be tweeting. (emarketer. com, February 2011). Many business professionals say Twitter is a great way to monitor what competitors and thought leaders are doing, stay informed of recent articles and blog posts relating to a subject of interest and get the inside scoop on what stories the media is researching.

Twitter users follow* people, organizations and companies of interest to receive real-time communications from these companies. Another way of using Twitter is to search for a keyword or phrase to sort all the tweets that mention the topic. Spend a little time reading the results and you can pick up on the topic-specific lingo and common hashtags. A hashtag is the # symbol followed by a key term, like #obama. Hashtags are used for more than just listening in on streams to identify influencers in a particular field. They allow conversations among fellow attendees at offline events and conferences to post messages. You may also see more TV News and radio programs mention a specific hash tag related to a topic of discussion. This provides an easy way for those interested in a specific topic to contribute, ask question or follow a conversation stream in real time.

Balmori Associates, the N.Y.-based landscape architecture and urban design firm hosted an in-person discussion of public space in its New York office with 40 Dutch landscape architecture students and their professors. In an effort to open the conversation to participants worldwide, Balmori Associates combined streaming video and Twitter, using the hashtag #mpplaces. The discussion used a Balmori project, the redesign of the public spaces in Balmori's own neighborhood (the Meatpacking District of New York's Greenwich Village) as the focus. The Twitter forum, with internal and external participants, narrowed in on the topics of shared space, urban decorum, context and public spaces' relationship between past and present.

"What I found of greatest value in Twitter was that it allows non-hierarchical comments; it did not become a debate of stars," wrote the firm's Principal Diana Balmori. The confines of 140 characters limits intellectual intimidation and as a result generates more input, because everyone relies on simple language to drive home their point. Participants were able to react instantly to the speaker's comments. Balmori continued, "Twitter diminishes the gulf between speaker and audience." Because participants are able to react instantly to shifts in conversation, "it increases participation by making everyone a speaker."

"Originally, I used Twitter to research information on various topics using hashtags," explained Kristin Worley, marketing facilitator of Woolpert, Inc. (http://www.woolpert.com/), a national design firm from Charlotte, N.C. "From that point on however, I realized how much value Twitter actually provided. I have used the articles and networking I gained through Twitter to guide internal corporate staff in their decision-making processes. Twitter also provides the opportunity for knowledge sharing among individuals, organizations and companies in the industry. Our marketing group has also used it to communicate with others regarding conference events, which is a great way to open more doors to conferences and tradeshows and further extend value to the attendees."

To help you get the most out of Twitter, try using TweetDeck, HootSuite or Sprout Social to organize those you follow into streaming lists. You can also use these sites to set up ongoing keyword and hashtag searches in an easy-to-see-it-all interface. The Twitter programs mentioned above can also help schedule future tweets, post updates to your other social platforms and monitor your influence and who your top influencers are.

We'll talk more about how you can increase Twitter followers and amplify your efforts in Chapter 3.

Who's On Facebook?

First and foremost, if you are a business you need to operate under a Facebook page, not a personal Facebook profile. We realize this frustrates many business owners who have already built up significant following under their personal Facebook page.

However, Facebook clearly states in its terms and conditions that profiles are meant for individuals and pages are meant for groups, businesses and organizations. In fact, if you have your business functioning under a profile rather than a fan page, Facebook can shut it down, and all of your "friends" will literally disappear. Trust us! This happened to a client who insisted on using a Facebook profile page rather than fan page.

It's understandable why people don't want to switch over to a fan page from a profile page; it takes time to build up friends, for one. Fortunately, in April 2011, Facebook added the "Profile to Page Migration" tool that allows you to easily convert your existing profile to a business page and all of your friends to "likes." We suggest you download a backup of your profile before making this transfer as there is no way to convert a page back to a user profile once you engage the tool, and since Facebook profiles function differently than Facebook pages, not all content and information gets carried over. We suggest that you visit http://www.facebook.com/note.php?note_id=214139221935487 to learn more about backing up your profile page and how to use the page migration tool.

Once you start operating under a Facebook page, you'll notice gathering friends, or "Likes" is a bit more difficult than when you are operating under a personal profile. In the beginning, you may have to make posts on your personal profile to encourage people to switch over and start "liking" and interacting on your new business page. With a Facebook Page, you can not directly invite people to "like" you anymore. Posting the Facebook "like*" widget on your blog posts and web site are other obvious ways to encourage people to "like" you and therefore join your fan page.

Although Facebook pages are slower to grow and may not give you the direct, measurable impact of LinkedIn, Twitter and a blog, it is still highly recommended to get started now. By 2013, 62% of web users and almost half (47.6%) of the overall U.S. population will be on Facebook (eMarketer 2011). And Facebook users are an active group with 50% logging in every day. In March 2011, Google changed its algorithm to give even more weight to social authority and online reputation. Now the number of "likes" a company has on Facebook directly impacts its overall Google ranking. Read more about Facebook group and fan pages in Chapter 3.

When Daryl H. Bryant released his new book *MS Living Symptom Free*, he turned to Facebook as a primary tool for building awareness and ultimately generating book sales.

"Social media was always a crucial part of the book's promotional and marketing plan", said Rania Eldekki of Hudson Horizons, (hudsonhorizons.com) an integrated web agency responsible for helping Bryant launch his Facebook page. "A Facebook campaign was initially developed to increase fan base and interaction within the MS community. As the campaign progressed, tactics were eventually directed towards increasing book sales," explained Eldekki.

Bryant himself was responsible for posting and interacting with participants on his MS Facebook community, helping to give it a more authentic voice than an outside marketing agency could alone. The passionate fan base of the Facebook page continues to grow, which has helped *MS Living Symptom Free* become a top ranked book on Multiple Sclerosis on Amazon.

How does this story help your business? By realizing that the use of social media, especially Facebook, is about building authentic relationships before you can close a sale. It takes a bit more time than a simple pay-per-click search ad, but the benefits are longer lasting and ultimately will decrease your client acquisition costs.

The value of a Facebook "Like" of your business or product is ultimately the value of that person's network. According to Facebook, the average user has 130 connections. Also, 29.6% of shoppers say they have discovered a new product after a friend has "liked" it on Facebook.

Getting To Know Generation Y (Your Future Employees/Clients/Vendors)

We believe that as older executives retire and the current college generation, which grew up with the Internet, moves into influential and decision-making roles in business, social media use will only expand. It's important to understand this generation and plan accordingly.

Generation Y, or the Millennials, succeed Generation X and include 60 million people born in the mid 1970s to early 2000s. Many of these are the children of baby boomers, so they are sometimes also referred to as the "echo boomers." This generation spans from young professionals to soon-to-graduate high school students, and most have been exposed to the Internet at an early age. On the whole, they are more computer savvy than any other generation. They are less trusting of corporate media, more likely to ask questions, more likely to share opinions online and they find word-of-mouth an essential part of gathering information. This generation is more likely to Google your company name and see what type of comments come up than to actually visit your company website. Ensuring that the right comments appear during this Google search, to ensure it reflects your brand, mission and goals, is very important.

Why Blog?

The best thing about social media is that it is highly flexible. Because you don't need to know any HTML, have graphic skills or know programming languages, it is easier and faster for most people to test, track and monitor the impact of different messaging, and to make changes in strategies and content development because of that feedback than a traditional website. This makes blogs an important tool for marketers, CEOs, client service representatives and anyone else facing the public in your company to get their messages out fast and efficiently.

Position your blog as the hub of your social media activity. By posting your ideas and company news to a blog, it not only gives you more space to develop your ideas (compared to a 140 character tweet or Facebook post), but also provides added search value and longevity of your information. (More on this in Chapter 3)

Like any communications vehicle, the best blogs write for a specific audience and purpose. Your blog can serve as the origin of the content for all other social outlets.

Christine Morris of Construction Specialties, Inc. explained how the company's vice president of construction, Howard Williams uses his blog ("People Centered Environmentalism," people-centered-environmentalism.tumblr.com) as a primary way to reach people interested in green building, chemical policy reform, or sustainability. "A blog is a perfect avenue for developing thought leadership in a specific area of expertise. Subscribing to a variety of blogs allows us to stay updated with the latest industry and market information, participate in discussions and voice opinions. Reading blogs written by well-informed "experts" in any given arena enable us to identify thought leaders that we may want to develop relationships with," explained Morris.

Blogs don't always have to be written by experts to be effective. In the case of the free, weekly publication, the *San Diego Reader*, blogging was used as a tool to build more loyal, local readers. However, instead of using staff experts or community leaders, they opened it up to any San Diego local who wanted to share stories, photos and thoughts happening in their own neighborhoods. The tactic helped get more localized content on the social web as the individual writers often shared their own stories with their social networks, in turn giving the *Reader* more exposure online. The additional contributions also helped the *Reader* generate more search engine friendly content, without putting extra burden on staff writers. Plus, the idea of allowing public blogging on a high traffic local web site lends itself to fun, sometimes-controversial conversations among locals which naturally increases the social influence and traffic of the *San Diego Reader's* primary web site. Read more about how the *San Diego Reader* set up their community blogs in the side bar testimonial:

Building community through blogs

"When the *San Diego Reader* (www.sandiegoreader.com), an alternative newsweekly, launched a new website a few years ago, it also launched a public blog section. Until that point, blogs were only authored by Reader staffers who had a weekly column in the print edition of the Reader. The staff-authored blog entries were carefully managed and went through an editorial process, just like any other editorial content.

"Given the nature of blogging, we were concerned that offering the public an open forum in which to blog would bring with it a monitoring nightmare. After all, profanity, libel, spam, racial epithets, and the harassment and abuse of others go hand in hand with giving people a space to freely speak their mind. For legal liability protection, and for our site monitors' sanity, we needed to contain the blog content, without hindering freedom of speech.

"Around the same time, the Reader's annual "Neighborhood Essay Contest" was getting underway. Therein was the solution. Giving the bloggers a topic to discuss would help contain the subject matter of the blogs. It would also provide a showcase for new writing talent to get noticed by the editors. Thus, the Reader's "Neighborhood Blogs" section was born.

"The public was encouraged to write about their neighborhood: the people, the places, the pets, how they ended up living there, how it's changed over the years, etcetera. The only limitation to the blog section was that the blog had to be about a San Diego neighborhood. As an incentive, three winning blogs were chosen each month. Winners received cash, and the winning entries were also printed in the weekly magazine.

"That was over five years ago, and the Neighborhood Blogs section is still going strong. The site still gets speckled with spam advertisements, libelous rants, and

inappropriate posts now and again. But overall, having a theme to the section has dissuaded many of those bloggers who may not have the best intentions in mind when seeking a place to post. Topic-driven content has helped contain the content tremendously. As an added bonus, the Reader has found some incredible writing talent through the Neighborhood Blogs. In fact, a handful of those neighborhood bloggers are now staff bloggers."

—*Jane Belanger, Consultant, San Diego Reader*

Differentiate Your Social Strategies

As you'll learn throughout this book, each social networking channel can offer a slightly different purpose in helping a company reach its goals. For example, YouTube can provide an excellent place to house company videos, while Facebook can serve as an ideal place to generate honest customer feedback and testimonials. Twitter can be quite effective for tracking customer's interest and monitoring what the competition is doing and posting your latest blog entry to Google+ can be an important tactic for search engine optimization. Blogging can be an excellent way to showcase your expertise on a particular topic, while Linkedin can help you find the right employees and vendors.

Now that you have identified your marketing goals, found your target audiences and have discovered a good mix of social tools to get the job done, next, you need to amplify those efforts. In the next chapter, we'll show you how you can increase your followers, fans, traffic and longevity of your online messaging.

3
AMPLIFYING YOUR COMMUNICATION EFFORTS

So you've set up your company Twitter account, launched the Facebook fan page, updated your LinkedIn profile and started a blog. Now what? How do you attract the attention of friends, followers and fans — and keep them interested enough to not only listen but also share your message with their friends, followers and fans?

Before we dive into the specific tricks and strategies that will help you reach your business goals via Twitter, YouTube, Facebook or other social sites, we want to stress that no matter which social tool you use, your messaging should be centered around encouraging engagement. Social networking is about making a connection with your online friends, fans and followers. It is about encouraging them to react, post opinions and engage.

Social media is not all about you. It is not about the latest press release your PR consultant posted on the newswire this morning or the big project you just landed last week. It is, however, about how these bits of information may affect the lives, family and friends of your audience. The information you post should be interesting, relevant and timely to entice your audience to react in some way, whether it is posting a comment, expanding on the idea, sharing that information with others or taking the desired business action you intended when you made the post.

Social Media is not all about You

The Ready Store (www.thereadystore.com), a food storage and emergency preparedness company, learns customers want to talk about themselves first.

"We started our efforts in social media during the booming period when every business was told they should get on the trend or perish.

We tried a lot of different methods for the first year — creating internal applications around Facebook and Twitter's API's, following hundreds of people - the works. We soon found however, that just pitching customers on our company was not getting us anywhere. We realized that the customer didn't want to hear about us, they wanted to talk about themselves.

We began to offer posts and links that allowed our customers to talk about themselves. They would be able to show off their own food storage and emergency preparation ideas. The more we allowed them to talk about themselves, the more engaged they became. Instead of posting about ourselves, we began to post about our customers in context of our business. This began to create an online community.

We began to operate under the motto that *the more we give, the more we get*. We began to offer daily prizes, in-depth articles and daily, relevant information on our blog. And the more consistently we gave, the better results we had.

Initially, instead of a direct correlation to sales, we saw a direct growth of customer loyalty. The more we showed them the true face of our company, the more they trusted us and wanted to buy from us.

We saw an increase in customer feedback, engagement, SEO and customers becoming evangelic on our behalf.

Overall, we grew by more than 100,000 Facebook followers in a years' time. We also grew to more than 13,000 followers on Twitter. We now have a larger online following than all of our major competitors and have a regular revenue income from our social media efforts."

—Brandon Garrett, Marketing Manager, The Ready Store

Other references:

www.facebook.com/thereadynation

@TheReadyNation
www.thereadystore.com

Practice Patience When Starting Your Social Media Campaign

As you try the tricks and strategies outlined in this chapter, keep in mind that developing a successful social media presence takes time and patience. Although you may not feel the immediate results as quickly as you could through a simple pay-per-click campaign*, social media outreach, when positioned correctly, will outlast any paid advertisement. In fact, each blog post, comment and tweet is still accessible by search engines long after your pay-per-click or other advertising campaigns have expired.

When you have something important to share or an opinion that sparks others to react, your message can grow exponentially. A company that steps outside of the box to post original commentary or even something entertaining or humorous will win out over the corporate blogger who continues to push out standard press releases and mission statements without creating an environment where people feel comfortable sharing or reacting.

Laura Davis and Larry Paschall, principals of HPD Architecture LLC (http://www.hpdarch.com) in Dallas, Texas say that engaging in social media is imperative to their firm's survival as a business. They decided to use social media to help HPD stand out from other architectural firms with the goal of bringing in work. However, as they entered the social media space, they started to see that building a solid online social network takes time and patience.

"We knew we could not expect to appear on social media outlets and have new clients start walking through our door, just as you cannot expect business to come to you just because you design a website or have a phone number," states Davis.

Like many other successful social media users, Davis and Paschall have discovered that it is not one specific tool that helps them discover and gain new projects and clients, but a combination of them. HPD uses a combination of blogging, Meetup.com, Twitter, LinkedIn and Facebook to reach their business goals of building awareness and establishing credibility as "talented, friendly and trustworthy architects in the Dallas area."

"Our blog has been essential in helping move our ranking up within Google" (Your ranking on Google determines how easily potential customers can find your company and related services online). "However, a blog does not stand alone and utilizing each social media tool in a combined effort has been the key ingredient in creating the results we have seen," says Paschall. "We have not seen clients come to us because we are on Twitter. But what we have seen are opportunities to participate in webinars for marketing companies, opportunities to speak at professional conferences, and opportunities to be a valued resource for a variety of companies."

Participate Unselfishly

As you begin to set up your own social media strategy, spend part of your time on the social networks unselfishly. In other words, spread your wisdom on Ask.com, Quora.com, LinkedIn or blogs to help others. Comment on other people's blogs, share your colleague's content, "like" other people's fan pages, and retweet other people's words. However, choose ways to be unselfish that are also related to your industry and overall business goals. While it is important to share information and other people's content, consistency in your own messaging will empower your social media campaign. Therefore, choose topics to share and comment on that are related to your own expertise so you don't confuse your existing fans and followers. After all, anywhere you post online has the potential to be found via search engines by potential clients.

"A lot of companies simply view social media tools as a means to promote and talk about themselves and their projects or products. Unfortunately, that is the quickest way to have their listeners tune out. People that follow a company on social media are looking for useful, relevant information." Davis and Paschall say.

In addition to participating unselfishly, it is important to be genuine. By engaging on a few of these networks you can use them to tap into your influencers and drive attention to your content, but make sure you don't robotically post the exact same update to Twitter, Facebook, LinkedIn and so on. "Each time we blog, we run through a process of social promotion where we share via Facebook, Twitter, Digg and StumbleUpon," says Scott Doyon, principal and director of marketing of PlaceMakers, LLC. "We also promote the blog post on Listservs where growth, development, environmental and community-building issues are discussed." For an in depth look at how Placemakers promotes their posts in order to drive readership and the thinking that underlies this strategy, read their case study:

Attracting Readership

Writing and posting a solid blog post is not enough. People still have to find it. Place-Makers' blog is written for a broad audience, so they use social media to share each post beyond RSS subscribers. Scott Doyan shares their promotion protocol.

Objective: To reach people in a lot of different places without imposing ourselves on them.

"We see place making through a pretty wide lens. We're building relationships with

environmentalists, developers, city boosters, bike and pedestrian advocates, foodies and all kinds of other folks who care about community improvement.

When we write a blog post, we try to put the broad-based interests of our audience at the center, which can generate comments where we might get a real conversation going. Or, it might not. It's hit or miss, just like life.

The traditional approach to marketing has always been to cut through all the clutter, get in the face of your target audience and have something of value to offer. It's not a conversation. It's a pitch. Your goal is to sell something and those who aren't interested tend to simply endure it because they know that's what you're doing.

Social media, however, is about conversations and relationships and that requires far greater sensitivity.

Our Strategy: To put ourselves out there and try to be useful.

Typically, one of the principals will write once a week. We do this not to promote our work (we rarely, if ever, discuss our projects) but to advance the larger community-building/smart growth conversation and to raise our individual profiles within that conversation.

Social media has become the engine that drives our readership because it's so efficient at breaking us out of our vocational silo of urban design practitioners and connecting with all kinds of like-minded groups with different agendas but similar end goals.

When we launch a new blog post, the first thing we do is to create a **bit.ly** link, instead of letting the page buttons create them for us. This lets us watch flow as we post to various places, and gauge the relative speed and interest.

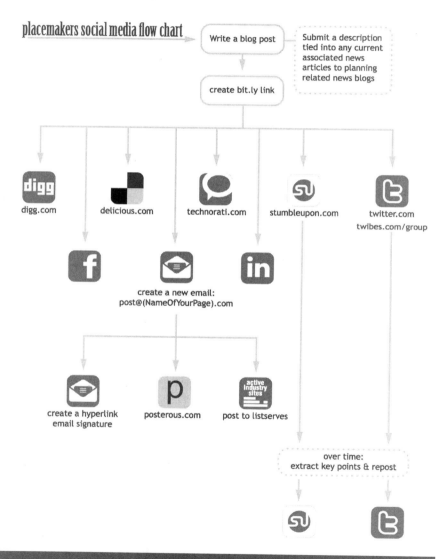

Figure 3.1: Placemakers Social Media Flowchart

Using that link, we create a short description of the post, that may only be two sentences, and:

1. **Digg** it.

2. Bookmark it on **Delicious** , providing a description, tagged with keywords, in the notes field.

3. Fave it on **Technorati**.

4. Recommend it on **StumbleUpon**.

5. **Tweet** it on Twitter and on **Twibe**

6. Go to email and create a new email to post@(NameOfYourPage).com. Paste the description and **bit.ly** link into the email. Send it to **Posterous**, where it posts as another, shorter blog.

7. Post to our various **Facebook** pages or any **Facebook** event page where it's applicable.

8. Share as an update on **LinkedIn**.

9. Add the title of the blog and its hyperlink to the **signature of our emails**, which is subsequently replaced by each new blog post.

10. Post to the **listservs** to which we belong, most of which are related to urbanism, community or architecture.

11. Over time, extract key points, and **Twitter/Twibe** them again, or write a note of them on **StumbleUpon**.

12. Write a slightly longer description, tying into any associated news articles and submit for entry to **Planetizen.com, Land8Lounge.com** and **SustainableCitiesCollective.com**, which are planning-related news blogs.

So sure, we promote things we're writing or doing sometimes but we don't make that our sole contribution to the conversation. We also promote things other people are doing. Or illustrate connections between seemingly disparate events. Or add a little levity.

Of course, there are still the more basic rules of etiquette.

- Don't inundate your mailing list or contacts with content.Be respectful of people's time.

- Don't comment on other people's blog posts with links to your own stuff.

- If you tweet, don't be solely self-promotional.

- Serve other people's interests, not just your own.

Additional Resources:

placeshakers.wordpress.com

www.placemakers.com

www.digg.com

www.delicious.com

www.technorati.com

www.stumbleupon.com

www.twibes.com/group/cityplanners

www.posterous.com

As you truly engage on these social spaces, you will realize that there is a different way to communicate with each of these groups. Take your different audiences into account and communicate with them the way they want to interact.

Case Study

Pretzel Crisps' "Social Sampling" Program Rethinks How to Connect with New Consumers

Objective:

Pretzel Crisps® wanted to introduce the brand to new consumers in a targeted and high-impact way. "We needed a groundbreaking, cost-effective way to raise brand awareness and attract new users," said Jason Harty, Director of Field & Interactive Marketing for Pretzel Crisps.

"By listening to the cloud of conversation and engaging with consumers in relevant dialogue, we could build increased interest in the brand and move Pretzel Crisps from an overlooked pretzel cracker to a sought-after brand in the competitive snack food category."

Strategy:

As a humble pretzel cracker, it's a pretty lofty goal to become a catalyst for social conversation, but that's how they started. By listening to and engaging in relevant conversations online, Pretzel Crisps delivered just-in-time product sampling to un-expecting new consumers. The brand refers to their innovative marketing tactic as "Social Sampling."

The regional field marketing teams use Social Sampling as a regular tactic during their daily routines. They search Twitter (primarily using advanced search) for 1) local tweets and 2) relevant dialogue. The search criteria are set to within 1 mile of their

location and they listen for a plethora of conversations. Having a party, going to a party, having a bad day, having a birthday, catching up with friends, simple love of cheese and so on...

There are dozens of conversations that would work for the brand to politely join and offer complimentary snacks. We're finding new ways to join the conversation every day. It's all about finding the right people at the right time who might be in need of a little snack. The perfect time to introduce them to Pretzel Crisps®.

We reach out to Twitter users by starting our tweets with @mentions so as to not spam the rest of our following. When we strike up a dialogue, we follow each other and DM the address where the local teams can rendezvous with the delighted recipient.

Results:

Here's a simple breakdown of the average number of people we engage with, and how:

If we reach out to 100 people via @mention with an offer for complimentary product:

- 25 respond back to us
- 23 of those people we connect with offline
- 22 people respond back online mentioning @PretzelCrisps, either via Tweet or blog post and many of them including incredible photos

Recently, one of our regional field marketing teams connected with the Marketing Manager at Funny Or Die via Twitter. What started off as a funny comment about

Valentine's Day and an overcrowded Red Lobster, quickly turned into a Social Sampling hit that reached over 3.1 million people. After listening to the comedy video website's Twitter conversations, the team saw an opportunity to engage and offered to hand deliver snacks to the office. The Marketing Manager was so grateful for the great snacks, he tweeted it from his personal page @schindizzle, as well as the company's page, @funnyordie.

The Social Sampling tactic has helped innovate Pretzel Crisps' field marketing approach and bring new users into the franchise by distributing over 13,600 samples via Twitter. Since the July 2010 launch of "Social Sampling," the brand has used Twitter to manufacture significant media impressions. By measuring the number of impressions generated from each social sampling interaction and the resulting reach through each user's following, Pretzel Crisps has garnered more than 17.5 million media impressions.

Social Sampling delivered earned media via tweets, blog posts, reviews and comments. While the brand has not been able to measure the specific sales lift, Pretzel Crisps continues to experience a growing sales trend and is confident that this hyper-targeted, high-impact sampling is creating new consumers each day. According to the 52 week IRI data ending December 25, 2011, Pretzel Crisps has grown 106% in Total U.S. Food sales from a year ago today.

Takeaways:

- There are no silver bullets.

- Genuine dialogue resonatesWe're all consumers and we're all about the right now. How can you deliver your message or offer just-in-time?

—Jessica Harris, Public Relations Director, Snack Factory LLC

—www.pretzelcrisps.com

Finally, once you post something online, don't abandon it. Listen and react thoughtfully to any feedback you get. Take time to reply to direct tweets andblog comments with a thoughtful response that will keep conversations going, rather than a quick "thanks for the comment!"

Make the Most of Your Offline Assets

Subject-matter experts are often drawn to traditional tactics for promoting their ideas and innovations, such as publishing and speaking publicly, as a means of advancing their practice and their profession. Professional service firms that see the upside of thought leadership and knowledge sharing as a way to build a highly skilled team and the company's reputation support and encourage these efforts. Social media's culture of sharing is a natural fit.

Perhaps you recently made a presentation at a local networking event. This presentation could drive the content of your next blog post — or two. Consider expanding on a couple of your points or posting an edited video of the presentation. You can extend this reach even further by tapping into affiliates and partnerships. Link back to your networking group's Facebook page or blog and mention the group @ name when you tweet about it. Follow your social promotions up with a phone call or email to select attendees or group leaders to ask if they would link to your blog post from theirs or to "like" your mention of it on your Facebook page or to retweet your tweet. (After all, these relationships aren't limited to digital discourse.)

We recently helped HMC Architects promote a white paper they had co-authored with Planetree, a non-profit organization that advocates for hospitals to adopt a holistic patient-centered model. "Design and the Bottom-Line" is a 21-page presentation of the benefits of incremental patient-centered design changes. Instead of just publishing the whitepaper and encouraging people to download and read it in its entirety, they created a 10-part blog series that expands on individual topics discussed in the paper-effectively extending the longevity of the message by 10 weeks.

HMC also began listening in on patient-centered and healthcare tweets and discussion threads on various LinkedIn groups to look for opportunities to share their patient-centered-design insights. When appropriate, HMC directed people to the whitepaper or to a particular blog post.

HMC's partnership with Planetree (http://www.planetree.org/) multiplied their efforts by tapping into the non-profit's communications network. Planetree also published the white paper on their website and promoted it in their own communications vehicles including an e-newsletter and their member community My Planetree. Planetree published a summary article in their monthly magazine Planetalk, and of course included it in Planetree's tweets, LinkedIn group discussion and Facebook page. This campaign was designed to not only position the authors, as well as HMC and Planetree, as a source of deep knowledge on this topic but also to reinforce the relationship between the two organizations. Figure 3.2 shows how partnering with another organization effectively extends the reach of the joint message in a targeted way and introduces the brands to the other's network.

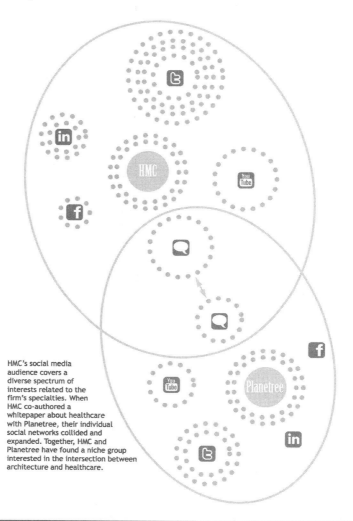

HMC's social media audience covers a diverse spectrum of interests related to the firm's specialties. When HMC co-authored a whitepaper about healthcare with Planetree, their individual social networks collided and expanded. Together, HMC and Planetree have found a niche group interested in the intersection between architecture and healthcare.

Figure 3.2: How partnering with another organization effectively extends the reach of the joint message in a targeted way and introduces the brands to the other's network.

Similarly, HPD realized the depth of their social network relationships would only benefit from taking the discussions offline. So, the firm created their own networking event, The Architecture Happy Hour, and leveraged the social network Meetup.com to drive attendance. Meetup is a global network of local groups with more than 7 million members in 45,000 cities. HPD uses it as a resource to find existing networking groups that fit their business and as a way to manage and promote their own. "By hosting and organizing the group, we connect people in the architecture and engineering community with synergy partners to whom they might not otherwise be introduced," says Paschall. "We also hope having the happy hour group will encourage other people in the community to start networking and start understanding that there is a value in building a business referral network."

How Often Should You Tweet, Post, Comment...?

According to a 2011 report from ExactTarget (http://www.exacttarget. com/), titled "The Social Break-Up," 90% of consumers unsubscribe, "unlike" or stop following companies because of too frequent, irrelevant or boring communications. [figure 3.3] In other words, the content of your messages is just as important as how often you push those messages out. Studies have shown that one update on Facebook per day is optimal, while you can tweet up to seven times per day on Twitter (as long as they are spread out throughout the day and not in quick succession. Too many updates is the quickest way to loose fans, followers and friends.

90% unsubscribe
posts are too frequent
posts are irrelevant
boring communications

Figure 3.3: The content of your messages is just as important as how often you push those messages out

According to the Edelman Digital Insights slideshow package released by Syomos on "Attentionomics Captivating Attention in the Age of Content Decay" (http://www.slideshare.net/EdelmanDigital/attentionomics-captivating-attention-in-the-age-of-content-decay), the massive growth of social media makes it harder for a firm's message to stand out. For example, of the more than 110 million tweets per day on Twitter, the report says that "each tweet decays almost as soon as it is released." According to Syomos, "92% of all retweets (and 97% of replies) happen within the first 60 minutes."

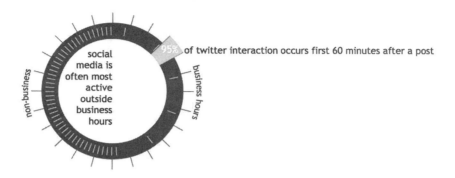

The same report discovered that in general, most Facebook users log in at the top and bottom of each hour. Similar studies have found that first thing in the morning, at lunch time and in the late afternoon and evening are the most active times on Facebook. This means that your post must gain some momentum (comments/likes) to keep it at the top of the list before and during these times. Keep in mind, though, that the "time of day" statistics are for the general population of Twitter and Facebook and not broken down by specific audience. Despite that fact, these statistics still serve as a great starting point and guideline to when you should start posting; however, as you develop a core following of your target audience, you may find a different time of day that is best to post. There are new social media monitoring tools like Timely by FlowTown, (www.flowtown.com) that will help you track reaction to your tweets and posts by time of day so you can understand what timeline works best for your company and goals. (Turn to Chapter 7 for more details on how you can track, test and monitor timing for maximum benefit.)

Consider The Benefit Social Media Plays Into Your Google Ranking

Don't get discouraged if you haven't had time to write a new blog post this week or that your latest tweet has already "decayed" just seconds after you posted it. Even if you don't get an immediate reaction from a post you've made, Google can still keep it alive long after you've moved on to the next message. Social media now plays an important role in helping you stay at the top of search engines. Esteemed search engines such as Google aim to provide users with the most relevant and up-to-date information. Therefore Google now indexes and displays tweets, YouTube videos and blog posts (sometimes even before your website). For more detailed information about search engine optimization (SEO) strategies, you can pick up a copy of co-author Holly Berkley's *Marketing in the New Media* or *Low Budget Online Marketing for Small Business*. (http://www.berkweb.com)For the purposes of social media SEO, incorporating keywords into your posts is vital to increasing the longevity of your social media efforts.

Here are a few tips to help your search engines find your social media efforts:

Keys for Search Engine Optimization:

Include keywords in blog title

Hyperlinc keywords instead of using "click here"

Include links back to your site whenever possible

Facebook: set up a "cause", "group" or "fan page"

YouTube Posts: list keywords in the description and title

Twitter: use keywords in your profile bio and in tweets

⚠ Keyword stuffing can negatively affect search engine rankings and turns off readers. Practice moderation. ⚠

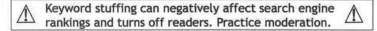

Figure 3.5: What works for optimizing keywords

- Incorporate keywords into the title of your blog.

- When blogging, never link back to your website with a "click here." Instead, use your keywords in the link. For example, "learn more about our San Diego Seafood Restaurant Locations." This gives the keyword term "San Diego Seafood Restaurant" more weight and helps your website's ranking.

- Don't use a Facebook profile for your business. These profile pages are password protected and therefore not visible to search engines. Instead, set up a cause, group or fan page for your business. (Information about converting your Facebook profile to a Facebook page was briefly mentioned in Chapter 2 and will be covered more in-depth later in this chapter.) In addition, consider your keywords when you select the name of your Facebook page.

- Whenever possible, always provide a link back to your website or blog (but remember the second bullet point about how to link back!). For example, use your website address in your signature when you post a blog comment. The more incoming links you have to your web site, the better your search ranking.

- When posting a video on YouTube, take the time to list keywords in the description, as well as use a keyword-friendly title.

- When using Twitter, use your keywords in your profile bio, and as often as possible in your tweets.

- Finally, don't over-optimize your titles and posts. "Keyword stuffing" can not only affect your ranking in the exact opposite way, but also make your customers less likely to actually read it. There is a fine balance between creating interesting, reader-friendly content and incorporating search-friendly phrases and keywords.

A Look At Amplification Strategies By Social Network

Below is list of top social networks used by businesses today. We've outlined strategies for amplifying your communications on each network.

Facebook

Give Facebook fans what they want, determining the right mix of content

A few years ago, we helped set up a Facebook page for CosMed Plastic Surgery Center, a medical tourism destination in Mexico. At first, the Facebook page was an after-thought to our other marketing initiatives as we mainly focused on SEO efforts and other social media activities (such as participating on various weight loss and plastic surgery related message boards where our potential clients often researched doctors). The Facebook page stayed at an even 200 likes for several months, with few comments. Most Facebook posts consisted of the same information that we just posted on our blog.

However with the explosion of social media, we quickly realized that paying more attention to the Facebook page and engaging with potential customers became a critical need, especially for something as controversial as plastic surgery in Mexico. As you can imagine, safety and trust are big issues when considering going to a foreign country for any type of medical care, so social media and real patient testimonials are crucial to helping new patients feel at ease and taking the next step to booking their appointments.

Figure 3.6: Facebook

No matter how informative the articles we posted to the Facebook page were, they were not creating the engagement needed. It was definitely a cold, one-way conversation. Then, we decided to launch a contest to increase awareness and engagement, plus gain a few great success stories from past clients. We used *Wildfire* to launch a video contest, where past patients could win $1500 towards their next procedure for sharing a video testimonial. The results were pretty dismal. In the end, the problem came from taking people away from where they wanted to be (Facebook) and making them try to figure out how to upload a video to YouTube through the Wildfire app contest platform. We underestimated the technical level of the audience and became tech support rather than marketers.

A few months later we tried again — this time, we made it as easy as possible for patients to share their photos and story — and to keep the interactions ON the platform they were already comfortable using. We sent an email blast to existing patients announcing the contest (same way we previously did, with same prize) only this time, because it was so easy, we immediately got success stories generating hundreds of likes and comments! The number of Facebook fans, which was at a stand-still for months, went up 775% in 2 weeks. Post views were up 500% and feedback 1,000% (**Important Note to Readers:** Be aware that Facebook is constantly changing the terms and conditions business pages must adhere to, and this may effect how you are able to run contests through the Facebook platform. Please refer to Facebook's latest terms and conditions before launching a contest on your Facebook page).

In addition to the new contest, we convinced the surgeons to start interacting with potential patients on Facebook. Now, potential patients could actually ask questions about surgeries and get responses from board certified plastic surgeons and a dermatologist. It added tremendous value to the Facebook page — and gave it a deeper, warmer level than an outside marketer alone could.

Beyond the contest and "Ask the Doctor" feature, patient to patient interaction was encouraged. The results of these transparent conversations have been invaluable. As a result, patients are expressing how much more comfortable they are booking appointments after talking with doctors and patients on the Facebook page.

Here's an example of just one of the Facebook comments exemplifying this::

"Awesome! I am excited for mine now. I was very scared before, but after talking with others who had it, I feel so much better."

Interaction with real patients and seeing genuine success stories really made a difference in putting potential customers are ease. Now we get posts like this one, asking for support:

"I have a consult coming up in January & am very nervous. Hopefully once I visit the clinic I will feel assured. Can existing patients please put me at ease? Thanks! Nervous Nelly in Cali."

Posts like this one are consistently greeted by an outpour of support from past patients, and provide potential patients with the feedback they need to book their appointment confidently.

Top 3 take-aways to help you increase your Facebook likes and improve Facebook Contests:

1. *Identify customer needs and give them what they want*

   In the case of CosMed Clinic, potential customers wanted two main things: the ability to interact with other patients and to be able to ask questions and get answers from board certified doctors in a medium they were most comfortable with.

2. *Hold a contest that is easy-to-enter and share*

   Take into consideration the technical level of your audience before you launch a contest in the social media space. Are they the type that would be able to easily create a video and upload it? Or would a simple text-based contest prove better results? Also, don't take participants away from the medium (for example Facebook) that they feel most comfortable using.

3. *Check in often and always answer questions as quickly as possible*

   The more exposure your page gets, the more you need to check it — multiple times per day, especially if you allow others to post on your wall. You are not only checking for questions and concerns from potential clients, but also monitoring any spam that may appear.

Converting Facebook profile to fan page

According to Facebook's terms of service, "Profiles represent individuals and must be held under an individual name, while pages allow for an organization, business, celebrity, or band to maintain a professional presence on Facebook."

A Facebook fan page is designed to become the official Facebook marketing presence for a business, but a business can also set up group or community pages for specific projects or discussions among a smaller collection of users. While fan pages are viewable by everyone on the

Internet, groups and community pages can be set up to be private or invitation-only. This makes them a good option for internal communications between employees or regarding specific projects or client groups.

If you've already built up a lot of friends on your Facebook profile, it's tempting to ignore the rules and use your personal site for business. However, Facebook has the right to shut down a profile that is being used by a business, and if that happens all of your friends will vanish with it.

There are advantages to having a Facebook page instead of a profile. One is the ability for search engines to find it and the other is access to Facebook's analytic tool, Facebook Insights. (More about Insights in Chapter 7.) With a Facebook page, you will also have access to the latest promotional tools, such as like buttons. You also have unlimited growth potential since Facebook doesn't limit the number of fans for a page. Conversely, a Facebook profile is limited to 5,000 friends.

Using Facebook Ads

A quick way to grow your Facebook fan base is by setting up a Facebook ad. Businesses can target Facebook ads to anyone on Facebook by geographic location, occupation, interests, ages and other key attributes. But keep in mind the more general you make your ad, the more expensive it will be.

Margo Schlossberg, Owner, Kura Design Handbags (www.Kura-Design.com) decided to try Facebook ads after she realized that her product had a slightly higher percentage of African American customers. She also learned that one of her popular pink and green handbags was the color of Alpha Kappa Alpha sorority. As a result, she created an ad with an African American model holding a Kura Design handbag, and used Facebook to target the ad to women in Alpha Kappa Alpha.

"The reason I chose Facebook was because of the ability to target schools, graduates, and interests etc," Kura explained.

Kura tested multiple calls to action and found that the photo of the African American model combined with the text "be the envy of your sisters" generated the highest click rate. The experience of using Facebook ads to target different groups made Kura realize the importance of audience targeting, especially for a small business when funds and resources are limited.

"It has become more important to be highly targeted. Selling bags as 'fashion bags' or 'wedding bags' has gotten so much more competitive as more and more online stores are targeting the same audience.

Targeting sororities or at least with this particular sorority, has seemed to work a lot better because it is so focused. You can easily find the chapters online and get a feel for which ones are largest. Additionally, girls show their 'sisters' so there is the opportunity for follow-on marketing once you get one in with the girls."

Provide incentives for liking your page

1-800-Flowers encourage customers to like their Facebook page by offering immediate discount codes. CosMed Clinic offers patients 10% off surgical fees just for liking the new Facebook page. And Fresh Brothers, a southern California pizza chain, incentivize Facebook fans by providing weekly coupons.

Other companies have similar promotions. If coupon codes and sweepstakes don't make sense for your business, try encouraging likes by giving away a white paper or access to some research or an article written by one of your company thought leaders. Offer value to your users.

Regarding the content of your Facebook posts, topics that do best on Facebook are those that make you appear friendly and thoughtful. For example, encourage others to join social causes or charities and also use humor in your posts. Tell stories, use emotion and keep conversations as genuine as possible. Even though your page is business-related keep in mind that people still do business with people. And don't be afraid to ask people to like you on Facebook. According to Journalistics, a blog that covers PR and journalism, (blog.journalistics.com), Facebook reported in 2010 that journalists who asked readers to like an article the user just read, had two to three times the activity of journalists who did not ask.

Whenever possible, use a photograph or graphic of some sort when posting to Facebook. This will naturally attract more eyes to your message. In fact, studies have found that Facebook posts containing an image will get 12 times the engagement compared to those without a picture. Also, consider an interesting profile picture that will help your posts and comments standout.

Take advantage of Facebook's interactive applications such as polls and quizzes — if they relate to your business and would be of value to your fans. Real estate developer Project^ gained most of their more than 800 fans from a simple competition using the poll feature on their Facebook page.

Read the Courtside Case Study sidebar for more information about how Project^ used Facebook to encourage tours and sign leases for an off-campus student housing community next to the University of Oregon:

Case Study

Firm: Project^, Portland, Ore, www.projectpdx.com

Project: Growing a Facebook fanbase for the Courtside property

Challenge: When Facebook is your marketing channel, organic growth is not always fast enough. The Portland, Oregon real estate developer Project^ explains how Facebook's interactive applications helped them quickly grow more than 600 targeted fans.

During the spring 2010 semester, Project^ was in the midst of constructing Courtside, a new off-campus student housing development across the street from what is now the Matthew Knight Arena on the University of Oregon campus in Eugene. With construction for the arena and Courtside happening simultaneously, there was little awareness of the new property or what this area of town would be.

The 176-bed Courtside development was scheduled to be completed in September 2010, just in time for the fall semester. The spring semester (during Courtside's construction) is the time when most of the leases for the upcoming fall semester are signed. Courtside needed to direct all interested lease signers to the website because there were no model units available to walk-through during this time.

Objective: To sign enough leases to reach a 95% occupancy-rate before the fall semester.

Strategy: Using Facebook as one of the many marketing tools, Project^ ran ads and interactive promotions to create curiosity and interest in learning more about the development. The first step toward attracting future tenants was to get students to click-through to the Courtside website and take a virtual of property. Getting students to like the page was also important to maintain interest through periodic promotions and updates on the construction.

Project^'s most successful promotion was a contest titled "The $1,000 Club Contest." With the help of San Diego, Calif.-based ad agency Farm they put post cards in the mailbox of every on-campus organization and emailed each club president to ask what their organization would do with a $1,000 donation. Courtside's Facebook page fans would vote on the submittals and select which club would get the prize. "We wanted this to be more than a contest," says Project^ Partner Anyeley Hallova. "We wanted this to help us create a sense of community and attract people who wanted to be a part of a community. By using student organizations we would be reaching groups of students that already shared a common interest." Since students had to like the Courtside page to vote, the club presidents asked their members to become Courtside fans so that they could vote for their club. The vote was held using Facebook's Questions feature and the contest generated more than 600 fans.

Lesson: The collective marketing efforts resulted in more than 80% of the beds leased by fall 2010. While this wasn't the 95% target, Project^ was still pleased with the results. The contest promotion generated likes from a broad sample of students and many click-throughs to the website - Facebook was consistently in the top four of website referrals — but obviously not all of the fans were interested in signing a lease. However, this broad fan base paid off again as the second Project^ property in the Arena District, Skybox, was being built.

The new property has 50% more beds, and benefits from a better awareness of the property's quality and the added foot traffic from the now completed Matthew Knight Arena. Instead of investing in a large campaign as they did with Courtside, Project^ was able to use the Courtside Facebook page to notify people about the new Skybox property and Skybox Facebook page. With a more grass roots approach, the Skybox page has more than 125 likes -a more accurate pool of interested lease signers. With Skybox opening in September for the fall 2011 semester, they are tracking to hit the same 80% occupancy by the time classes start in 2011.

Going forward: Project^ now uses the Facebook pages for both properties to communicate directly with tenants and students considering signing a lease in ways that encourage a stronger sense of community within the property. For example, Project^ uses the Facebook Questions feature to let residents discuss on the communal items available to everyone such as music preferences for common areas, magazines subscriptions, board games and which products they should stock in the vending machines. Personal referrals are the top way for getting new leases and these often happen on Facebook, so it continues to be an important place to for Project^ to connect with future tenants.

Resources:

http://www.projectpdx.com

www.facebook.com/livecourtside

www.livecourtside.com

www.liveskybox.com

www.facebook.com/liveskybox

www.livearenadistrict.com

Finally, take advantage of the news feed. This is where most Facebook users get their content. You want your post to stay on each user's news feed for as long as possible, to generate the most exposure. Fortunately for small businesses, Facebook's news feed algorithm doesn't use how many fans or friends you have to decide whose post stays on top longest. Rather, posts are prioritized by three things: how recent the post was made, how recently a user interacted with it, and how many likes the post received. Therefore, encouraging comments by asking questions and keeping the conversation active is beneficial to the longevity of the post.

LinkedIn

As mentioned earlier in this book, participation on LinkedIn means doing more than just setting up a profile and uploading your resume. This applies to both personal and company LinkedIn pages. As of March 2011, more than 90 million LinkedIn members have set up a company LinkedIn page to promote their business. Even if you haven't proactively created an account for your business, there may already be one on LinkedIn. This is because LinkedIn's business directory pulls basic company information (such as number of employees and history) from content collected through its partnership with BusinessWeek. That means that when you view a personal LinkedIn profile, the name of the companies referenced in that profile usually links to a company page.

Figure 3.7: LinkedIn

LinkedIn uses member information to supplement the basic facts and as a result the bulk of the data on company pages is derived directly from member profiles who indicate themselves as an employee. This includes statistics like new hires and recent activity (based on recently added and modified affiliations with the company) or comparative charts between the company and an average of its competitors.

Small businesses that take control of their LinkedIn company page have found another opportunity to drive home their brand personality, showcase their portfolio and validate their work and expertise. Pages allow users to add things such as the company logo, description, website address, Twitter handle, RSS feed and even embed YouTube videos or a news module that displays recent headlines of articles that include your firm. Like other social channels, LinkedIn also has its own set of analytics for monitoring the effectiveness of your page. With a little more effort you can connect your blog and your tweets to your page or even upgrade your account for a monthly fee of about $195 to allow you to post job listings.

As you set up your company page, take the time to fill out the "Services" section. By providing a lot of keyword friendly information here, it will be easier for potential customers, employees and partners to find you. It's also a good idea to solicit recommendations from your clients. Overall, the more complete your profile is, the better it will serve you.

If you've finished setting up your company page, click on the "Promote my company" link. LinkedIn continues to update this section with tools and targeted ad buy opportunities to help you promote your company page.

In professional services, clients are drawn to your firm because of you or your employees and LinkedIn is an excellent place for relationships to be sustained and grown. That is why it is so important to make sure that in addition to your company page, your personal profile is as complete as possible. Also, since LinkedIn pulls information from member pages, the company page will not accurately reflect the current state of your firm if a good percentage of your staff doesn't participate. Therefore you should encourage employees to participate on LinkedIn.

Consider the best keyword phrases that you want to be known for and use these same phrases throughout your profile and bio when appropriate. This will help people better find you through LinkedIn's search.

Your professional headline is perhaps the most important piece of your profile. This is what people will see first when they are searching for someone with your skills. By default, your profile headline will be your most recent position or job title. However, you can manually change this to whatever you want. Take time to craft a statement that will not only help you stand out but also describes your strengths while using your keyword phrases.

Also, be sure your LinkedIn URL includes your name. This will help people better find you online. Your LinkedIn URL should look resemble http://linkedin.com/in/yourname. In most cases you will need to manually set this up. Simply log in to your profile and scroll down to where your "Public Profile URL" is listed. Click the "edit" button to enter your name. If you have a common name, one that is already taken, you may need to add a middle initial or perhaps a period between the first and last name.

Be sure to take a look at the list of LinkedIn applications. LinkedIn frequently adds new ones to help you further promote your profile and messages. Start with using the applications that connect with your other social accounts like Twitter and WordPress. Using these applications will help you easily integrate your most recent post or tweet into your LinkedIn profile and out to your LinkedIn connections.

Once you have your profile set up, do a quick search on LinkedIn for groups related to your industry and areas of specialty, where your target audiences may be. Interacting within these groups will help your company stand out among your target audiences. The more you show off your expertise in a group by providing valuable information, the more users will see you as a trusted expert. This will help build your online brand.

Twitter

First of all, don't get caught up in the numbers on Twitter. There are paid services where you can gain hundreds to thousands of twitter followers. However, as a small business owner, your goal should not be about how many Twitter followers you have, but who those followers are.

Figure 3.8: Twitter

Find potential customers you want to target by searching for keywords or hashtags* related to their interests. Next, find your competitors and see who follows them and who they follow to get more ideas. Where Facebook provides a more personal connection and people are more selective of who they "friend", with Twitter it's okay and completely acceptable to follow and be followed by many types of people, most of whom you have never met.

It's also a good idea to follow companies and services related to you. And if you are a local business, definitely follow the local business groups, tourism pages and media. This will help Twitter better categorize you, and you'll be more likely to show up when potential clients search under "Who to follow".

"Follow Friday" is another popular way to discover interesting new people to follow. On Fridays, many users send out tweets with "FF" or "#FF" and then a list of @names to indicate whom they think others should follow because of the value of what they have to say.

Once you have your list of followers, an easy way to get a specific user's attention is to retweet (RT) them or call attention to them using their @name. It is also common to use "MT" instead of "RT" when retweeting a long tweet and abbreviate it to allow space for your own comment. If expanding your Twitter influence is part of your social media strategy, commit to spending a few minutes each week to retweeting someone. Choose someone with a list of followers that represent your target audience. Make sure to add your own comment or perspective in front of the retweeted message to show a bit of your own personality and perspective. If you are lucky, they may retweet or reply to your next post — exposing your tweet to their followers.

You can also reach out to a Twitter follower privately with a direct message (DM). To keep people from abusing this, direct messages are only available between users who follow each other. You can send a follower a direct message, but if you don't follow them back they cannot respond to you via direct message.

It is essential that you fill out your Twitter bio. As people search and look for new people to follow, many look only at your bio, in addition to your latest tweets. Make sure your bio says something interesting enough that will make someone want to follow you. Let them know exactly what kind of expertise you provide or information you will be tweeting and provide a link to your blog or website. And if you are a local business, include your city.

Hashtags are not only useful for listening in and searching, they are also a great way to get more eyeballs on your tweets. You aren't the only one streaming tweets that include a particular hashtag. Once you find the people who are talking about a particular hashtag or key word, look for opportunities to engage. Contribute something interesting to a hashtag stream and you are likely to gain a few more followers or find a future customer. Read the Pretzel Crisp sidebar for how this company has used Twitter to find samplers for their product and double their sales.

Hashtags are also used as a way of connecting your tweet to a bigger conversation happening in a tweetchat*. These are scheduled Twitter events where people tune into a particular hashtag at a particular day and time to participate in a moderated discussion. Tweetchats that are related to your industry or subjects related to your business can be a great place to learn from others and offer your own insights.

Finally, when you are seeking other Twitter users, for the purpose of hoping they will follow you back, try reaching out to those individuals who follow more people then they have following them. These people are more likely to follow you back. Common etiquette is appreciated on Twitter, so welcome new followers with a direct message or mention them in a tweet that thanks them for following you, but make sure you personalize it so that they know it isn't an auto-generated message. It's also nice to follow people back.

YouTube

According to a February 2011 comScore report, more than170 million U.S. Internet users watch online videos. However, there aren't a lot of small businesses taking full advantage of YouTube or Vimeo yet.

Figure 3.9: YouTube

Start a YouTube or Vimeo channel and upload any company videos, presentation clips or media interviews about your company. When Bob Kelleher started The Employee Engagement Group consultancy in 2009, his Generation Y daughter advised him to post a YouTube video to promote him as a keynote speaker. So he pulled together slides from his presentations that would help potential clients understand his subject matter and then set it to music. His first video titled "What is Employee Engagement" now has more than 13,000 views and his second video, "The Ten Steps of Employee Engagement" has almost 10,000 views.

Kelleher notes, "The key thing with social media is the 'viral' aspect of social media marketing. If you have the right key words, and the right product, people find you." In fact, his videos have directly resulted in unsolicited keynote inquiries from prominent local companies and businesses as far away as Warsaw, Poland.

He also gives the video a lift by incorporating it into his other marketing and communications efforts. Since he owns employeeengagement.com, linking to the video is a natural fit, he also has linked to his videos in his email newsletter that goes out to 4,000 people and he also uses the videos and encourages attendees to visit his YouTube page in each of his keynote addresses.

Having all of these videos uploaded to a branded company channel not only presents an organized video portfolio, but helps each video promote each other. For example, as a potential customer finds one of your videos, your other videos show up in the right hand bar. As you upload your videos, be sure to write a detailed description for each one, keeping your keyword phrases in mind. Google owns YouTube and often displays videos in addition to text search listings, so this is another opportunity to make your listing stand out.

Keep videos short. Thirty to 60 second videos are ideal for most watchers. You may think you need a longer run depending on your specific goals, but in most cases, anything more than five minutes is really too long. With a YouTube account, you are able to not only track how many views your video is getting but see exactly the point in your video where a viewer stopped watching. This will give you a good indication of how long is too long and which pieces of your video are not interesting.

Think you can't afford a video? Get creative. Buy a flip camera for under $200 and make your own video, or have a videographer on elance.com or odesk.com animate a video for less than $300. Or hold a contest where customers create the videos about your brand for you.

Blogging

Figure 3.10: Blogging

Blogging provides an excellent opportunity to develop more thoughtful opinions and to share insightful information, as it naturally allows more space than a short tweet, comment or post. For most business leaders the content they post on their blog is the core information that they then promote throughout other social tools. For instance, a company may post a blog entry with an article about a new project. After the blog is posted, they can use Twitter and Facebook to post a link to the blog and provide a snippet of what the entry is about.

Unless your blog is meant for internal eyes only, don't use an internal company blog system or custom built blog software for your blog. If you do, you are not taking advantage of all the social aspects and networking opportunities available. Having a blog on a blog network, such as WordPress or Blogger, opens you up to an entire network of related blogs. Plus it makes life a whole lot easier, as you have access to the latest promotional tools.

Simply go to wordpress.com or blogger.com and sign up for a free blog. You'll be ready to post your first article in 20 minutes. Blogs not only give you an easy way to update your customers on new projects and company news, they also present the opportunity to gain free search traffic. Blogs help search engines find your site because blogs are largely text based (which search engines love). When you've titled your blog, categories, articles and posts using your keywords they naturally lend themselves to link building (giving easy ways for people to share content). Plus, your blog will be a part of the WordPress or Blogger network, which also helps build link popularity and exposure as the title of your blog will automatically appear on other blogs related to your topic.

Although you can use a blog for updating product and service information, think about using it to build relationships and expand your brand. Express options, and seek comments and feedback.

Here are a few other ways to promote your blog:

- Seek similar blogs (that don't compete with your business) and post comments when you have something to add. When it's relevant include a link back to your blog. The key to doing this right is to post something of value. If it sounds like spam or seems as if you are just trying to get a link, the owner of the blog will likely remove your post. Always aim to add value with everything you post online. People don't have tolerance for blatant spam. In addition to posting, you can also contact the blogger directly and exchange blog posts for a week. This opens you both up to new audiences.

- Ask for comments. Blogs are designed to be commented on, so close your blog with a question. Encourage people to give opinions. Sometimes being a little controversial is a great way to spark comments and make your blog go viral! And once you get some responses, provide follow up posts and answers related to the person's question. Keep the dialogue going as long as possible.

- Give some thought to the title of the blog post. Take time to craft an attention grabbing title along with an interesting photo. (You can purchase stock photos for a few dollars at bigstockphoto.com). Using keywords in your title will not only let search engines find you, but will also help your chances of showing up in the feeds of other related blogs in your network. In addition to the keywords, the headline should be written to encourage readers to click.

- For more insight, read how one blogger, Anjali Shah grew her blog, the Picky Eater, through social media:

Not all social network audiences want the same thing: Understand what your audience wants on each social network.

Anjali Shah, food writer and owner of The Picky Eater, a healthy food and lifestyle blog learns what her audiences want on different social networks, and posts accordingly.

"My goal has been to grow awareness for my blog, The Picky Eater, and my passion for healthy food in the most lightweight manner possible. Since I was starting from scratch and didn't really have a budget to work with, I relied on all forms of free marketing — which mostly involved social media. I wanted to increase visits to my site, increase engagement of the readers on my site, and increase the number of subscribers/followers I had.

"I use all forms of Social Media to market my blog, from Twitter to Facebook to Pintrest to LinkedIn to Google+ to FoodBuzz. Social media is my primary (and only) form of marketing. I post engaging content for my followers to all of these sites regularly (at least daily, and often more than once a day). I also use social media to make connections with brands or other influencers that I admire, follow or love.

"My lesson learned: While my blog is mainly about food, I found that people really wanted to make a connection with me personally: they wanted to know more about who I was, where I come from, and what it would be like to get to know me. I realized that social media is a great outlet for a more personal connection with my followers — so instead of muddling my brand on my blog (by including random tidbits about me that have nothing to do with food), I've focused that content more to my social media outlets. It gives people a reason to follow me on Facebook or Twitter — because they get something more out of it than just seeing when I update a blog post.

"Social media has been instrumental in growing my blog. Before I became active on Facebook, Twitter, etc. (which was about 7 months ago), I had 300 Twitter followers, 18,000 page views a month, and 100 Facebook fans. Today, I have 1,055 Twitter followers, 100,000 page views a month, and 900 Facebook fans. Using social media effectively has enabled me to exponentially grow my blog to a place where it can truly turn into a business."

—*Anjali Shah, Blogger, The Picky Eater,* [www.pickyeaterblog.com/]

—*As told to Shireen Gupta, Melrose PR* [www.melrosepr.com]

Figure 3.11: Google+

Google+

At the time of writing this book, Google+ is still in its infancy. Its user base is the smallest of all of those mentioned in this chapter. The primary users consist primary of technology and marketing professionals. However, with that said, we do advise that you start a Google+ page for your business. Why? Because its Google and it could just change the way consumers search and find businesses in the very near future. We are already seeing friend's faces appear next to relevant searches of companies they've +1'd. Its adding a whole new social layer to search that is sure to expand as more and more people adopt the social site.

However, as a small business owner with limited time and resources, we don't expect you to spend your precious social networking time here. (Especially as Google is still working out many of the bugs with the new social network) Instead, start by using your Google+ account as a place to simply re-post your latest blog or company information to give your SEO a boost. Focus your online relationship-building on social networks where more of your customers already interacting.

Yelp

For local businesses like hotels, restaurants, shops, hair salons and any other business with a local address hoping to get added foot-traffic, Yelp is essential. More than 32 million Yelp users per month are searching for new businesses (primarily on the go, with their mobile phone) and writing reviews about their experiences.

Figure 3.12: Yelp

First, go to Yelp.com and see if your business is listed. If it is, be sure your profile is complete. Add photos, hours, and a complete description with your keywords. Next, read your reviews. Yelp allows businesses to privately or publicly respond to all reviews, good or bad.

If you get a bad review, it's a good idea to reach out to that person privately and establish that human contact. Be kind, no matter how frustrating or wrong the review may be. Find out if there is anything you can do to improve the customer's experience. You could offer a discount on the customer's next visit in hopes they will re-post a nicer review. Many times, simply reaching out and letting a disgruntled customer know they have been heard is all they need to remove or change their post about your company.

However if all else fails, and the negative post remains, you'll need to ask your loyal customers to post more positive reviews. The goal here is to outweigh the negative reviews and get your "star" count back up. This type of outreach is easier if you've built up a loyal following on the other social networks, like Facebook and Twitter. Ask your fans to help you out, by writing a review about their experiences.

"For anyone just getting started with social media marketing, keep in mind that your attitude is the most important consideration," states Christine Morris, communications and special projects coordinator with Construction Specialties, Inc. in Muncy, Pa. "If engaging in this type of work is a chore, you're likely not going to get much out of it. Go into it with a sense of adventure. Do your research, watch, listen, join the conversation and have fun with it!"

Still feeling overwhelmed? Let your employees help. The next chapter shows how businesses can use their most valuable asset, employees, to catapult their messages on the social networks.

4
ENGAGING YOUR MOST VALUABLE ASSET: THE ROLE EMPLOYEES AND CUSTOMERS PLAY IN YOUR SOCIAL MEDIA STRATEGY

It still amazes us how many corporations actually block the use of any social media use during work hours. According to a 2011 openDNS study, 14% of companies blacklist or block Facebook from company computers — compared to only 1% blacklisting pornography sites. However keeping employees from engaging on social networks can prevent a company from leveraging its most powerful assets — knowledgeable, creative and passionate employees.

When you allow employees outside the marketing department to get involved in online conversations, your brand has the ability to provide real insight and valuable conversations on projects and expertise related to your business goals. These conversations naturally go beyond pushing a PR crafted mission statement. Your employees can be the key to your authentic voice. These conversations help humanize your brand and build real relationships with existing and potential clients in a way that direct mail or other one-way conversation channels just can't.

So unless your employees, clients and business partners are engaged in top secret projects, let them talk about it! Chances are, you're working on some very innovative, creative and exciting projects that you want to promote. Allowing your employees and other stakeholders to share openly about projects and experiences they are most passionate about, lends itself naturally to exciting, genuine and viral content on the social web. And everyone from project managers, to business development, to human resources can get involved in the social space.

"It's the ideal way to highlight the people who drive our firm forward. We're more than BIM models and calculators; we're also the people behind the work: guide dog raisers, teachers, philanthropists and music videos performers," explained Michael Pinzuti, web manager at structural engineering firm Thornton Tomasetti. "Social channels allow us to share, promote and celebrate exactly who we really are. If the firm's website represents the polished front-door view of the company, social media represents an open window allowing a richer understanding of all the dimensions of who we are and how we work."

Identifying Internal Social Media Collaborators

If you are leading your company's social media program and internal contributors aren't knocking down your door, you may need to seek these individuals out. For businesses — especially those with multiple offices — communicating within the company's internal networks is essential for coordinating your external social media effort. The Corporate Communications department at global architecture firm and social media early adopter HOK began its "Life at HOK" blog in 2008 by connecting with the firm's global HR network. They asked each office's HR department to nominate a blogger for their location. There are likely many internal communities bound by some common interest or shared goal within your company.

Multi-directional communications tools like Microsoft SharePoint or an internal blog support employee collaboration and information sharing. These internal tools borrow from social media to help build internal networks and to foster idea sharing and collaboration. Facebook-like functions allow employees to personalize their profile and update their colleagues on their projects and perspectives.

Such internal or closed social networks, lend themselves to targeted, niche-oriented collaboration and sharing. Mimic Technologies, Inc, a Seattle based robotic surgery simulator company, developed the dV-Trainer to help surgeons improve their skills on the *da Vinci* surgical robot. In addition to reaching out via the traditional social networks to reach their target audiences, they also launched an employee/client driven social network with Salesforce Chatter (www.salesforce.com/chatter/). The private online community was developed for clients and key industry influencers in robotic surgery to share and discuss how they are currently using the dV-Trainer. Those in charge of teaching residents robotic surgery can upload their dV-Trainer curriculum directly to Mimic's Salesforce Chatter community called MShare http://www.mimicsimulation.com/training/mshare/, where others can comment, and "like" it. An extremely niche community like this allows collaboration on a highly specialized subject matter, and helps position Mimic Technologies, as well as the surgeons who use the product, as leaders in their industry among their peers. It also serves a customer service need, as peers can share ideas, help recommend new curriculum for the dV-Trainer and the right employees can easily weigh in on any problems or concerns that may arise.

Free blogging sites like WordPress.com make it easy to create a private blog for "internal-eyes" only, without having to depend on IT. WordPress, by default, is meant to be a public forum. However you can also use it internally by opting to protect your posts with a password or keep them completely private. Simply click on the edit link next to "Visibility: Public" under the "Publish" options, to select the desired visibility for your posts.

Aside from supporting the basic communications needs of the company, these tools can be a gold mine for someone tasked with leading social media for a business. Tap into these (as a contributor and as a listener) they can be a spring of ideas, knowledge and possible resources for your external social media efforts. The culture of social media is about engaging and sharing. It only makes sense to start with your own community of employees. By leveraging internal communications tools to grow your network of resources and ideas, the external social media program you create can make the most of the ambitious and authentic personalities within.

A good way to get a sense for who is inclined to be your external social media accomplices is to find out who is already personally using Facebook, LinkedIn, Twitter, etc. Some internal communications tools have a survey function built in. If yours doesn't, applications like Survey Monkey make it really easy (and free if you keep it short) to survey and monitor results quickly. This information can be a valuable benchmark for future surveys or data to track your progress.

Share your findings internally as a part of a campaign to keep social media in the front of their minds. Reach employees who haven't adopted the internal tools yet by using other internal vehicles, like

for internal eyes only:

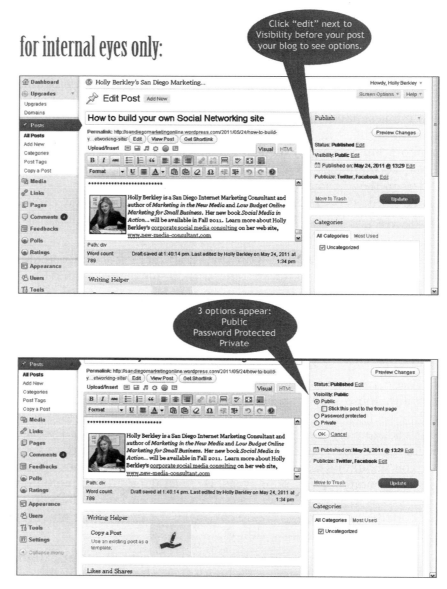

Click "edit" next to Visibility before your post your blog to see options.

3 options appear:
Public
Password Protected
Private

printed posters hung in common areas or an email blast. Make sure each communication about your social media program invites them to participate in the "behind the scenes" efforts that go into creating the external content.

Ask staff to "like", "follow", subscribe or join the company pages and accounts — and ask them to refer their industry friends/contacts to the accounts as well. Make your external social media objectives clear and include information on how they can participate.

As you populate your external blog and other networks with new content, use your internal tools to encourage employees to comment and share posts, by posting hyperlinked headlines. Share external social media accomplishments with the group. Pass along complements to your contributors through these visible internal channels "Jane Doe's opinion blog post was picked up by three widely read blogs, drew six thoughtful comments and we saw a 66% spike in blog traffic."

Internal communications tools are also great resources for sharing your upcoming external social media plans. Let staff know what topics you are researching for future external blog posts through an editorial calendar that sets some preliminary dates for when you'll be blogging on a particular topic and allows staff to submit projects or ideas to you in advance. Ask your readers specific questions to help you develop these, i.e. "Does anyone know a source for this type of research?" or "Have we used this technology on any of our projects?"

Keep your eyes and ears open for internal mentions of material that could be repurposed. This could be presentations that have been given at events or conferences, articles or whitepapers that an employee has written, general research that was conducted for a project or even popular internal conversation threads. With a little work these can be broken down into singular ideas and repurposed as blog posts, or cleaned up and made available on your company's YouTube channel and then promoted through Twitter, Facebook or LinkedIn.

In most companies, subgroups are popular activity centers. Collectively these can be a wealth of information, ideas — and sources. Take stock in the people who are most comfortable engaging internally and the topics they gravitate toward. These could be subject-matter experts with knowledge to share or simply people who are comfortable sharing feedback and extending conversations in social forums. Contact these people individually to consider ways they could be helpful outside the firewall as well. Encourage them to contribute a blog post, submit a comment, man the Twitter account or even just to forward interesting data and articles that are worthy of tweeting or posting.

Connect with the undercurrent of ego that may be present among certain employees (and even clients) by aiming the spotlight on individuals. This can pay off in their loyalty and interest in helping you the next time around.

For CosMed Clinic, a plastic surgery center, their past clients are their most vocal promoters. When given the opportunity, these happy clients share before and after photos, post advice to other's considering surgery, and even make plans to connect with each other in the real world. They do this all via the CosMed Facebook page. As their social media consultant, we identify who the key influencers are the Facebook page, and take their success stories to the next level in the form of a blog post, pitching to media, or in the form of a YouTube video. These clients typically welcome the opportunity to get their success story highlighted further and help in the sharing of the story to their social networks.

In social media marketing, selecting the best client, or even employee, for highlighting online often goes beyond who may have the best "before and after" photos, but rather who may have the biggest social network of friends and family who may continue to share that story in a genuine way. For CosMed Clinic, one of the most viral client success stories was based on a client who underwent post-bariatric surgery (after weight loss surgery). We posted the story to the CosMed Clinic blog, but she was the one who ended up sharing the post with her weight loss support groups, which lead to a record number of reads and shares for the blog post, among a very targeted audience.

Strength In Numbers

One of the benefits to empowering employees, business partners and even clients to tweet, post and chat on yoru companies behalf, is numbers. You can simply cover more of the massive social web when you have more adovates commenting on your behalf.

Matt Hames, Manager of Media Communications of Colgate University empowers the Colgate Alumni network to help the college gain further exposure among its target audience. In fact, the group worked so well together during a recent Twitter effort, they were able to trend nationally via a #ColageDay hashtag. With millions of twitter users collectively sending more than 100 million tweets per day, getting mentioned as a trend on Twitter gives you excellent additional exposure for your business.

"We use Twitter to engage Colgate alumni. We talk to alums, interview them on Twitter and post news about the school. When we asked them to help us trend on Twitter, it worked! On Friday the 13th (aka Colgate Day), we managed to get #ColgateDay to trend nationally on Twitter." See Colgate's side bar to understand how they leveraged their alumni group:

Strength in numbers helped Colgate University's Alumni Network Trend on Twitter

"We use Twitter to engage Colgate alumni. We talk to alums, interview them on Twitter and post news about the school. We also asked them to help us Trend on Twitter, and it worked.

On Friday the 13th (aka Colgate Day), we managed to get #ColgateDay to trend nationally on Twitter.

Colgate was started by 13 men, with 13 dollars and 13 prayers. The address is 13 Oak Drive, 13346 (13 + 13).

The mac-daddy of 13's is Friday the 13th, which has evolved into ColgateDay.

For Friday, we thought: can we overwhelm Twitter at 13:13 EDT with Happy ColgateDay tweets?

We created this page to talk about the plan. www.colgate.edu/colgateday.

We also printed business cards (attached) to promote the event. We left them around campus as an effort to increase intrigue. The overall goal is to get 400 new followers by the end of April. We're also focusing on current students since if we get them following now, we'll be able to keep them engaged after they graduate.

We posted reminders. We tried to make it a call to action: "Are you in?" with a link to the site. The website had 512 unique pageviews and was only promoted on Twitter. You can't find it unless you heard about it on Twitter.

The week of the event, we sent an email to alums.

Cut to the day of the event. I didn't believe for a second we would trend, but I did think we would have fun trying. We would all be invested in something that is on Twitter. That is a powerful result for social media. Getting people truly invested.

With more than 100 million tweets per day, the odds were slim. I would guess we needed thousands. Thankfully, when our small army took on Twitter, other people re-tweeted it.

We think trending for the right reasons is a way to engage alums and grow the community."

—Matt Hames, Manager of Media Communications,
Colgate University http://www.colgate.edu

Keep Marketing Goals in the Forefront

No matter who leads the voice of social media in your company, the person in charge of marketing and sales voices should always play a vital role in it — even in the background. In the case of CosMed, although the clients appear to take center stage in much of the social media efforts, as their marketing consultants, we are still monitoring conversations happening via Facebook, and helping to instigate and direct conversations in a way that fits into the overall sales and marketing goals of the company. This can include highlighting relevant posts, getting doctors at CosMed involved in a specific conversation or sharing key bits of health or medical information to spark further conversation.

In regards to employees chatting and posting on behalf of your company, no one should be unleashed on the social web without a strategic plan, crafted in sync with the goals of your company and its marketing and communications groups. Just as corporations have brand guidelines that establish logos, colors and tone of voice, so should you spend time to craft social media guidelines that any employee who engages on the social web should adhere to.

Conscious Box, a monthly subscription service that introduces subscribers to ethical, sustainable, and healthy products, encouraged all of its employees to participate on the social web.

"Everyone is encouraged to participate, but we ask they leave the tough questions to me or one of the other founders," explains Jesse Richardson, Co-Founder and Chief Content Officer/Chief Marketing Officer of Conscious Box.

"The biggest problem we face is subscribers not understanding our shipping layout and structure. They get angry if they order a day after our cutoff, and may even lash out on public forms or on our wall. The main thing we would suggest to other small businesses is this: first, don't be scared to remove offensive, extremely sensitive comments. We don't advocate censorship, of course, but our regular subscribers don't appreciate rude comments. Beyond that, be open, honest, and transparent. Luckily, we haven't had any problems with employees on social media. The best thing to do, we've found, is to really imprint the idea that the employee is working as the voice of the company ­ so be mindful, cautious, and creative." (**Read more about Conscious Box's use of social media and how they involve their employees in the side bar**)

How Conscious Box employees and Founders use social media to build awareness and alleviate customer concerns

"As Co-Founder and Chief Content Officer/Chief Marketing Officer for Conscious Box (a monthly subscription service that introduces subscribers to ethical, sustainable, and healthy alternatives), I handle about 90% of marketing related social media efforts regarding consumers. For the B2B side of things, we position Jameson Morris, the CEO and co founder, as the figure head.

For us, a young startup (began in October of 2011), social media has been the key driver of sales. We primarily use Twitter, Facebook, Pinterest, and Instagram to develop our brand identity and communicate the mission and philosophy of Conscious Box. For us in the environmental niche, authenticity is critical, so developing a daily narrative is essential for incited patronage and trust.

Outside of Conscious Box, Morris and I also co-own Organic Soul, a holistic health and wellness communities on the web. We have leveraged this community in support of Conscious Box, but Organic Soul itself is a separate entity. Our readers and subscribers are not kept in the dark, of course. This, in fact, adds to the level of authenticity required for our market. We build this primarily through word of mouth, attending trade shows, pamphleteering, and some very low level social media budgets. We do, however, spend a considerable amount of time targeting social influencers, bloggers, and YouTube personalities, often trading physical product for review.

Measuring success comes in two platforms: new subscriptions and social share of voice. We don't necessarily look at Klout or reach, but rather the number of direct referrals back to our site. For this, Google Analytics is key.

Regarding employee engagement, everyone is encouraged to participate, but we ask they leave the tough questions to me or one of the other founders. Our Instagram, for instance, is managed by an outside employee. He lets us know when there is a question he can't answer, and I hop on and figure it out. Regarding guidelines, we ask employees to imagine what they want to hear from customer services proper grammar and syntax, a generous but non-awkward use of smileys, and prompt responses. We also ask they speak from the "we" prospective.

The biggest problem we face is subscribers not understanding our shipping layout and structure. They get angry if they order a day after our cutoff, and may even lash out on public forms or on our wall. The main thing we would suggest to other small businesses is this: first, don't be scared to remove offensive, extremely sensitive comments. We don't advocate censorship, of course, but our regular subscribers don't appreciate rude comments. Beyond that, be open, honest, and transparent. We had a major problem with a shipping courier last month and after dealing with subscribers as courteously as possible, we received a number of sympathetic, very supportive comments.

Luckily, we haven't had any problems with employees on social media. The best thing to do, we've found, is to really imprint the idea that the employee is working as the voice of the company so be mindful, cautious, and creative."

—*Jesse Richardson, Co-Founder and Chief Content Officer/ Chief Marketing Officer,* Conscious Box

www.consciousbox.com

Companies like Zappos boast more than 500 employees using personal Twitter accounts to help promote the company's ideals and products. And Best Buy bravely empowers more than 150,000 of their employees to join customer conversations throughout the social web. And we are now seeing more small and medium sized businesses follow suit. No matter what size business you have, guidelines must be put in place before allowing any employee, whether its 1 or 150,000 loose on the social web. After all, anything posted, commented on or tweeted is public and forever online.

Employee Training

Take time to train your staff on social media best practices as well as what they are encouraged to talk about verses what information should not be made public. This could range from the distribution of an official policy and a list of dos and don'ts, to formal training sessions as official and comprehensive as you would any other type of in-house training. You may even consider hiring an outside social media training consultant to help you develop and set up guidelines to best fit your company's value, goals and mission. After all, how your employees talk about your company, will be in the public eye.

Nokia, the mobile phone manufacturer, requires employees to complete a six-part social media certification before they can become active on the social web. While Best Buy is able to successfully manage its 150,000 customer service and tech reps using social media by ongoing training and conferences.

As you look to develop your own guidelines, here are our top four recommended rules that will benefit your company:

1. **A list of Best Practices**

   Develop a list of social media best practices. Take pieces from the list we have created at the end of this chapter, as well as add a few that may be central to your company's brand and mission. Make sure all employees who post anything to the Internet on behalf of your company are aware and understand the list. Companies like Best Buy provide a list of best practices to each store, so employees would better know how to communicate with customers in the social space. A well-thought out list of best practices will be crucial to avoiding a potential PR or legal nightmare that can occur as a result of an employee posting an inappropriate comment online.

2. **Separate personal and professional accounts**

   We recommend asking employees to create separate accounts for work-related interactions (for example twitter). This helps reduce confusion when employees start using their social profiles to post pictures of their family vacations for example. In FaceBook for example, you can have one company page, and make key employees an "Admin". This way they can post information directly to your company FaceBook page outside of their personal FaceBook profile. However, keep in mind that customers can still click an admin picture to see employee personal profile pictures, bio and names of groups that employee belongs to. (The employee's personal newsfeed and/ FaceBook posts stay private unless the employee "friends" that customer). This overlap of personal and professional profiles is why making sure all employees follow the best practice lists is so vital. Let employees know that even items posted on personal blogs and profiles, reflects their professionalism as a whole. Remind employees that everything gets connected in some way, and comes back to the company image.

3. **Ongoing Training and Open Discussion**

   Social Media continues to grow and expand with new rules, widget, tools and sites popping up almost daily. We recommend periodic meetings with your contributing staff to talk about new trends as well as let employees share their ideas about what's working and what's not. Then adjust your guidelines accordingly when appropriate. Social media is a constantly changing medium, and your guidelines should be designed to be flexible.

4. **Make it easy for employees to engage in a consistent way.**

   Take a tip from Best Buy's social media tool kit and have your marketing team help employees with profile pictures, and provide them with company logos and approved imagery, so that anyone posting on your behalf has a consistent look.

5. **Define Your Goals for Employee Engagement in Social Media**

   Part of your employee training should include defining an agenda for why you are allowing them to be on the social web in the first place. Is it to share knowledge and expertise? Demonstrate values and leadership in your field? Gain real feedback to improve existing projects? Or to build relationships in hopes of attaining more future business?

Once you define these goals for social media, realize that not all employees will or should engage on the social web in the same way. Take inventory of the strengths and weaknesses of certain individuals to determine the best way they can use their time on the social web. For some employees, the most valuable thing they can do will be to listen to the social web. By setting up Google Alerts with keywords around the projects they are working on, they can gather real time information and conversations as they happen online, and report back to their group. Employees can also play a role at "amplifying" positive conversations that may help move projects or company influence along. After they discover and identify specific conversations, encourage them to re-tweet or comment on posts to give it more leverage and extend its shelf life on the social web.

Choosing the Right Employees to carry the company Voice

When we were asked to set up a social media strategy for Lake Flato, a San Antonio, Texas based architecture firm, the first thing we did after sitting down with the principals to define the objectives and overall goals of the social media campaign, was to interview their staff. We asked a range of employees from marketing coordinator to graphic artist to IT to architects questions about their existing social media use and interest. We also asked about their unique backgrounds both professionally and personally as well as about groups and affiliations they belonged to and were active members of.

Our goal was to identify employees with a genuine interest in communicating on behalf of the company via the social networks, as well as those who could provide a fresh, thoughtful perspective that was still in alignment with the company's overall mission, brand and goals. Plus, it helps to identify employees who already have genuine ties to existing social networks, affiliations or groups that can mesh well with the overall goals of the campaign to help propel a new social media effort more quickly.

Advising on the right employees to help carry the voice of Lake Flato in the new social media program was made easier when we learned that the company had already set up an internal community with SharePoint that was run by staff. They proudly called this internal social network FlakeNet. Here the staff posted awards, upcoming industry events, as well as "lessons learned" and important documents needed for client projects. But in addition to a learning and work resource, it also became a place to post personal announcements about office sporting events, birthdays and engagements. They even post humorous pictures such as staff celebrity look-a-likes and "guess who's baby picture this is?". In the process, the staff was able to find a common way to bond, and get to know each other. The fact that this information was not for the public eye, gave staff more freedom to express themselves and their opinions, and essentially form their voice within the company. Choosing the right voices to carry the Lake Flato message to the public becomes a bit easier when you see how staff engages on the private forums.

Recommended Employee Guidelines

Employee guidelines can vary based on your industry, business objectives and brand. In order to help you develop your own, we've pull together some of the best employee guidelines from a variety of industries (many are posted online for public view) of top companies like Best Buy, Dell, Zappos, Nokia and others to bring you a list of important social media guidelines and best practices your company should implement before allowing employees to use the social web on your behalf.

1. **Only engage if you can have a constructive conversation.**

   In other words, not all posts related to your project or industry need a comment. Recognize the difference between an angry community member's rant about your designs for an upcoming development and a concerned resident that just needs to understand the project better.

2. **Engage only when impact can be made.**

Strive to add value with each engagement. "Engaging in online conversations is a tremendous opportunity for highlighting the thought leadership activities taking place at the firm" writes Nick Bryan in HMC Architects' Social Media Policy. "Be sure that what you're posting adds value to the practice of architecture and is promoting the firm's values." Always adding value includes sticking to your area of expertise. Employees should only be encouraged to comment if it is in an area they specifically work first hand.

3. **Be transparent. Be yourself. Be smart. Be respectful. Behuman. Be professional.**

These are the key traits we see on social media policies and that we agree are important characteristics for engaging in social media. All posts should always be kept in a positive tone, and respectful of others — especially competitors.

More and more, employees will have their own blog or web site outside of what they are doing for the company. HMC addresses this issue with the following statement:

"Ultimately what you post is your responsibility, so be sure it reflects you positively. Please make it clear to your readers that the views you express are yours alone and that they do not necessarily reflect the views of HMC, our clients or your coworkers. To help reduce the potential for confusion, we would suggest the following notice — or something similar — in a reasonably prominent place on your site (e.g., at the bottom of your about me page):

"The views expressed on this site are mine alone and do not necessarily reflect the views of my employer."

Many bloggers put a disclaimer on their front page saying who they work for, but that they're not speaking officially. This is good practice, but may not have much legal effect. It's not necessary to post this notice on every page, but please use reasonable efforts to draw attention to it — if at all possible, from the home page of your site."

4. **Indentify what information should never be made public**

Work with your legal team and speak with your clients to understand which issues should not be discussed. In the Thornton Tomasetti (TT) "Social Media Dos and Don'ts", the firm encourages employees to "Understand what can and cannot be talked about. Things said in passing in the hallways at TT are not necessarily open for conversation outside the firm. When in doubt, treat it like the nuclear football. A good test: Will this information help us help our clients?" In general, it's important to ask staff to think before they post and run any information that may be sensitive by a designated marketing or communications leader. Along the same lines, make sure imagery you post is approved. Best Buy actually provides approved logos, widgets and other social media tools for its employees to use to avoid an inconsistent brand look.

5. **Designate Times when Employees can use the Social Web during work hours.**

We saw a few best practice lists that state "Don't let social media activity interfere with your work". It's a good idea to set designated times when you allow employees to use the social web. Many companies that allow employees to engage only do so outside of normal business hours. Our advice? It really depends on your overall goals, and many times, you want to comment when conversations happen. Sometimes, waiting until "after business hours" is too late.

Be sure to have a Google Alerts or other social media tools in place that at least one key individual is in charge of, and who can alert the right internal people who should provide comments. Also, as you read Chapter 7, about measuring and tracking your social media program's effectiveness, you will be able to understand if there is a better time of day when employees should be posting.

5
EXPERT POSITIONING

While an expert positioning strategy can be used to help your company sell specific products, it is especially critical for businesses in the professional services industries. As a professional service firm, your company's reputation is reliant on the knowledge and success of the individuals you employ. In fact, this is a primary reason we often push marketing an individual ahead of the company brand in social media marketing campaigns.

The importance of leveraging an individual's reputation in a firm became crystal clear to us during the research and writing of this book. In one case, a client happened to be seated next to us on a cross-country flight just days after a well-known company had announced that it was acquired by a larger firm. The client admitted, "I don't care if the firm is owned by someone else. I don't care what the name on the sign is. I will continue to do work with the business as long as the person I trust is there. If he moves on or retires before I am able to get to know and trust someone else. I will go somewhere else to work with a person I know I can depend on."

Through your projects and daily work, you build trust and expertise with your clients. Social media provides a way to enhance those relationships and keep client bonds thriving long after a project is complete. Keeping the relationships alive via social media helps establish long term trust which in turn opens your company up to future business with that client, and ideally, will open your company up to that customer's trusted social network as well.

In the past, industry thought leaders were established through numerous speaking events, published works and featured interviews in industry publications. However, thanks to the social web, you can start building your reputation as a thought leader right now.

But before we get started, let's be clear. Not everyone has what it takes to become an industry thought leader. Being an expert in one's field goes beyond simply sharing links to articles others have wrote, posting your latest accomplishment to Facebook or joining the latest LinkedIn Group. All of these social media tactics are useful for marketing your business and keeping it in the forefront of your client's eyes, but do not necessarily qualify you as an industry expert or thought leader.

Online experts are motivated by a genuine curiosity in their field and continue to ask questions, develop new ideas, and share knowledge that in turn, helps them develop a loyal following. In social media, loyal followers share your ideas with their social groups. The more exposure you get for your contributions to the industry, the faster you can become a recognized expert.

According to Francesca Birks, Senior Foresight and Sustainability Consultant with global engineering firm Arup, those who find the most success in establishing themselves as thought leaders are those who are most comfortable in leadership roles. These individuals have the confidence to develop and support innovative ideas and have the ambition to be a part of shaping the future of the company.

"These people want to spar intellectually. These are people who see the big picture and understand that there is more going on beyond the day to day of winning work and pleasing clients," explains Birks.

Investing In Multiple Thought Leadership Roles Within Your Company

While in the past, thought leadership roles were left to the CEO and company founders, today's social media channels make room for many levels of expert voices, including employees with unique or specific skill sets and knowledge bases. These potential subject-matter experts are employees who thrive when given the opportunity to share ideas, and need a fresh stream of innovative thoughts and conversations to be fulfilled professionally. Companies that give this type of employees the possibility and support of the firm's resources to become subject-matter experts are betting on the potential of these individuals --as change agents and as leaders.

For some the concern of promoting an employee over someone who has ownership in the company is risky. The thought of investing money and brand equity in an individual only to have them walk or be lured away by the competition, is too risky.

However, Chris Parson, founder of knowledge management software and related technology services firm Knowledge Architecture, is an advocate for more people to take on the role of thought leader. He notes that "Thought leadership is a team sport. It's about asking questions and posing ideas." Social media is a fantastic forum for this.

Birks also advocates reaching out to others to build a solid thought-leadership campaign. "There is no way 11 people can be responsible for all thought leadership for our company" she says. In order to cover more of the social web and keep conversations relevant, Birk's company inspires colleagues and friends to help share ideas, ask questions and participate in their thought leadership campaigns.

Become a Part of the Conversation

Just as social media can be a powerful tool for amplifying your communications efforts, it is an equally powerful listening tool. By joining a LinkedIn Group and following specific Twitter hash tags related to your industry and expertise, you can keep up to date on new projects and concerns of your colleagues. Or to offer your expertise directly to potential customers and clients, post thoughtful answer to questions in support forums. The surgeons of CosMed regularly demonstrate expertise while building awareness of their plastic surgery clinic by posting answers to health, beauty and weight loss questions within relevant online communities.

Google Alerts is an easy way to get notified anytime the media, an online community or other web sites is discussing a subject that makes sense for you to weigh in on.

You can take this idea of social media listening even further by using a professional social media listening or monitoring tool. Just type in "Social Media Listening" or "Social Media monitoring tools" on Google and you will see plenty of options. Or, for bigger companies hoping to cover more ground, use a more advanced listening and monitoring tool like Radian6. Such tools will allow you to discover your industries hottest topics and most pressing problems and concerns. The tool works with keyword phrases and will provide you with direct links to conversations happening that contain those phrases. Then you can weigh in as an expert on those threads, and start building your credibility.

The goal, as Birk explains, is that in order to be a leader, you have to be a part of the conversation. And if you aren't the best person to answer a question posed online, pull in your employee or other team member who specializes in that area. "We've looped some team member's personal blogs into the framework" says Birk.

"You have to be part of a conversation if you want to be a leader in it. The alternative is that other people will crowd the space and fill the void," says Birk.

Steve Mouzen of Mouzen Design and Founder of the New Urban Guild agrees with using social media as a tool to grow and expand on ideas. As a promoter of the tenets of New Urbanism and practical sustainability for years, he has a firm grasp on the role of a thought leader. Steve has created and nurtured his network and tapped into their common interests by sharing his ideas and useful information through workshops and networking groups. Social media came along and made all of this easier for Steve.

In one of Steve's blogs, Useful Stuff (http://usefulstuff.posterous. com/new-media-for-design-types), he wrote "Social media is working magic that was unimaginable a decade ago. Once, we read the daily newspaper, watched the evening news, and followed the American Top 40. But over the past decade, we've learned how to speak to ourselves again."

He went on to write, "commenters on my blog posts regularly have great ideas that improve the ideas I was blogging about. This is an enormous time-saver, because I can't possibly bring all their experience to bear on the question... because I don't have their experience."

In our interview with Steve, he advises that anyone hoping to position themselves as a thought-leader become a part of a cause and promote a set of ideals, as opposed to promoting their own pocketbook. He explains that great ideas need networks in order for them to spread. Today's social media tools allow a way for ideas to form and spread faster, more efficiently, to more people, and in a way that just wasn't possible 10 years ago.

"For example in the past we'd share ideas by hosting a workshop with about 100-150 attendees, " he explained when asked how he communicated ideas before social media. "But today, social media allows us to engage a larger group. The Facebook page for the Original Green has more than 1000 members".

Another way to demonstrate your commitment to your area of interest is to help advance the understanding of it. Research is a great way to discover more about a subject. Explore areas that can strengthen your own services and products. If it's useful to you, chances are others will be interested in learning about it as well. Social media is a great place to formulate your hypothesis and test it within your professional circles. By allowing others to participate in it and help shape your thinking you create ambassadors who are willing to spread the word.

There are obviously many ways to conduct research. Use your blog as a means of publishing the research and your other networks to let more people know about it.

For a simple approach, you can use Facebook's "Question" tool to ask your friends and fans a question. LinkedIn also has a "Poll" function that can feed into your Twitter and Facebook accounts. These tools are designed to take your poll viral so that people who respond can pose the question to their network and the members of their network can pass it along to their connections, and so on. The question, its results and any comments are stored on your page for anyone to view, but shorten the link and a fewer-than-140-character summary and it becomes a conversation starter.

If you have more time and resources, you can create your own experiment – online or offline – and tap your social networks to drive people to participate.

Architecture firm OWP/P, which is now Canon Design, partnered with German furniture manufacturer VS and Canadian design thinking firm, Bruce Mau Design, to study the role of the learning environment in educating children. The resulting research became a book of 79 ideas for transforming teaching and learning, *The Third Teacher*. In the book, the final idea was for the reader to "add to this list" and this request spawned the creation of a website, blog and other social media outlets to interact with readers and ideas. (http://www.thethirdteacher.com/)

People are captivated by new findings related to their work and problems. Structure your undertaking in a way that is fair and doesn't hint at a bias. You may even want to hire a research consultant to help make sure you are aren't doing anything to skew the results. As you promote your findings, don't forget to position your blog as its hub.

By virtue of carrying out the effort you position your name at the center of your findings, but by adding your personal take on the results, you demonstrate your grasp on the topic as it stands and where it is heading. Your assessment of your research findings may just be the basis of a bigger publishing opportunity – like it was for *The Third Teacher*.

Writing a book is no doubt a lot of hard work, but the resulting credibility and pool of content for future speaking, writing and social media undertakings could be just what is needed to springboard your business to the next level.

Read the sidebar from publicist and author of *Celebritize* Marsha Friedmanto learn why you no longer need a publishing house to present your ideas to the public.

Establishing yourself as a Thought Leader through Book Publishing

Many writers know the story of "The Christmas Box" — and I'm not talking about its inspiring message of love, although that's nice, too. I'm referring to its provenance.

Richard Paul Evans wrote the novella for his daughters in 1992 and made 20 copies, which he gave as Christmas gifts to friends and family. The story was so enthusiastically passed along, he offered it up to six publishers. They passed. So in May 1993, Evans self-published and distributed the book locally, in Utah, himself.

Two years later, Simon & Schuster paid Evans the largest advance ever by a traditional publisher for a self-published book — $4.2 million. And the rest is history.

I share this 20-year-old tale to address a concern sometimes raised by new authors when they call us here at EMSI. After we promise to get them exposure in newspapers and magazines, and interviews on radio and TV shows, I'll often detect a pause on the other end of the line. And then, "But I'm self-published. The media may not be interested in me."

Oh, baby, the media doesn't care!

The stigma of being self-published disappeared long ago. Heck, J.K. Rowling — the big kahuna of authors — is self-publishing her new e-book version of the Harry Potter series. The son of famed romance novelist Barbara Cartland is self-publishing the manuscripts that remained after her death. I could go on and on with the names of celebrity authors who are self-publishing, and new authors who've become multi-media darlings and popular sellers.

Now, it's important to note: None of these people published books that look like they rolled off a conveyer belt in the garage. They have beautiful, eye-catching covers and they're well-edited and free of errors. Most important, all of these authors spent a lot of time and/or money promoting themselves.

There's no stigma when it comes to self-publishing, whether you go with print, print on demand, or e-book. But you won't be well-received by the media — or book stores — if your quality is less than professional.

With 22 years in this business, I've lived the publishing world changes. To me, the tide turned when Amazon.com set up shop in 1995. The online bookstore turned the industry on its ear by removing the greatest barrier between millions of would-be authors and their dreams of selling books: distribution. Simply put, before Amazon, people bought books in stores. And the only way for authors to get into the major chain stores was through traditional publishing houses.

Those publishing houses were very selective because it was their money being invested in publication.

Amazon gave self-published authors and the small presses their first mass marketplace, and a whole new industry of publication options soon followed. Traditional publishing houses responded to the increased competition by cutting back the numbers of titles they produced, further limiting new authors' access to that avenue. Today, more than 75 percent of new titles are either self-published or from non-traditional publishers, and more than half of buyers order their books online or through something other than a bookstore.

One thing that hasn't changed, whether a book's published traditionally or not, is the author's responsibility to market him- or herself. At the big publishing houses, it's mostly the best-known celebrities who get help in that department. Everyone else is on his or her own. Of course, that goes for authors who've taken the non-traditional route, too.

Amanda Hocking, self-publishing's newest wunderkind at age 27, has racked up more than $2.5 million in sales since she started selling her paranormal romances as e-books in April 2010. She did it, she told USA Today, through aggressive self-promotion on her blog and through Facebook and Twitter. Writing in a genre that's extremely popular with young adults hasn't hurt, she added, and she worked her tail off — she had 17 novels written when she started publishing.

So, will the media or consumers hold it against you if your book is self-published or not with a major publisher? Absolutely not. That's the way of the publishing world today, and everybody with a hand in it knows that.

Will they turn up their noses if your book looks like it was written, edited and designed by amateurs? Yes, frankly, they will.

If you do everything the way you should — write a fabulous book and hire a great publishing team to professionally edit and design it — can you become the next Richard Evans or Amanda Hocking?

Yes you can — but only if people know about it.

—Submitted by Marsha Friedman,
CEO of EMSI a national Public Relations agency,
www.emsincorporated.com,
and Author of *Celebritize Yourself*

Its important to note that just because self-publishing is an option, does not mean it is best, or the right choice for everyone. In the example of Amanda Hocking, although she was successful with self-publishing, she eventually signed a multi-million contract with St Martins Press, a traditional publisher, after deciding it was too time-consuming to do the writing, editing, distribution and the heavy promotional work it takes to market yourself, and a book.

Building your Fan Base

Thanks to social media, Marcela Abadi Rhoads, owner of Abadi Accessibility, an accessibility consulting firm, is one of only 500 Registered Accessibility Specialists in the country and is considered an expert in the field. Her active presence in social media has lead to her being contacted by a publisher, which ended in a book deal. She is the author of "The ADA Companion Guide" which explains the 2010 ADA Standards. As a result of her book and continued use of social media outreach she is sought after by facility owners designers and buildersacross the country who look to her for guidance to understand the accessibility standards.

"Social Media is a way that I become the 'expert' in my field," she explains, "The more that I post information about architecture and accessibility and the more I engage in discussions in the same area, the more exposure I get and the more credibility I receive."

Her approach to social media is to be an "open network and accept everyone." In other words, she always follows those who follower her on Twitter, accepts every LinkedIn request and FaceBook friend request. "The more people I connected with the more exposure I get," she says, "It is sometimes surprising who I am connecting with. You really never know who might be a good referral source. My book would not have happened if it wasn't for my efforts with social media."

Using a Blog for Expert Positioning

Today, it seems like everyone has a blog. In fact, according to Blog-Pulse, there were 152 million blogs on the Internet at the end of 2010 and that number is expected to grow. However, having a blog does not automatically make you a thought leader.

In addition to posting thought-provoking, conversation starting, innovative ideas within your industry, you need to establish a loyal following to help you extend the life of that idea, and continue to grow your audience. Unless you have a book, a speaker series or some other way to communicate ideas with large numbers of people, building a blog is the most efficient way to get your ideas heard and should be the center piece of your thought-leadership campaign.

A blog is an excellent place to share ideas and pose questions and get conversations started. However even the best written blog still needs a marketing strategy behind it. And the social web lends itself perfectly to promoting blog posts. Free blog services like WordPress. com and Blogger.com come with widgets that allow you to easily connect your blog to Facebook, Twitter and popular social news web sites to make sharing your most recent blog post easy.

Leverage Existing Thought Leaders' Blogs, to Promote your Own Ideas

A good way to start generating quality traffic to your new blog is to seek similar industry blogs that your target audience is already reading. Make sure the blog topics and their authors complement your overall goals and brand, rather than compete for services. Once you've identified some good blogs that fit this description, determine which ones have the most traffic and therefore, should demand more of your efforts.

Web sites like Statsaholic.com, Compete.com and Quantcast.com allow you to type in a URL and see how much traffic a blog gets. You can also see what types of audiences visit that blog by a demographic profile break down. Web sites like Quantcast.com even show you what other web sites that audience visited immediately before or after that blog, which can give you more ideas on potential web site to reach out to.

Once you've identified the top blogs that your target audience is reading, get involved in the conversation. You can post a comment with link back to your blog, which should help you gain targeted traffic. However the key to doing this right is to post something of value. If your comment or post sounds "spammy" or that you are just trying to get a link, the owner of the blog will likely remove your post. Always aim to add value with everything you post online. People don't have tolerance for blatant spam and posting anything that could be mistaken as such will hurt your efforts to establish yourself as a thought leader.

In addition to posting a comment on another blog, you can also contact the blogger directly and exchange blog posts for a week or schedule regular "guest posts". This opens you both up to new audiences and gives your blog more depth. Another idea is to interview the popular blogger and post an article about him/her on your blog. By promoting that blogger, he might promote your blog to his audience in turn.

Get Conversations Going on Your Own Blog

Blogs are designed to be commented on. They are a great place to share ideas and even argue. Consider blogging on topics that are some-what controversial, that can encourage a positive and intellectual debate. Its also a good idea to ask for comments. Let readers know that you value their input and want them to comment.

Whenever you do get a comment on your blog, make sure you respond directly and publicly to that person. It's not only polite, but it also helps keep the conversation going. Instead of simply saying "thanks for the post!" ask another question and try to keep the comments flowing.

Another strategy to help build momentum for an important post is to go back after a few weeks and post a follow up. This helps build up link popularity and exposure for the first post.

Finally, develop a thick skin. Not everyone will love all your ideas. Putting yourself out on the social web as a potential thought leader can open you up to public scrutiny. And once in a while, you will get comments that are unflattering. Fortunately, as the author of the blog, you can choose which comments are made public. You will be tempted to hide all the negative comments, but in our experience in social media this is a big mistake. If voices don't feel like they can be heard on your blog, they will stop reading. Let the negative posts go public (even if you have to edit them a bit). Then be confident about your ideas when you rebuttal and address that reader's concerns. Having a few negative comments and responding with grace and knowledge shows honesty, concern and helps build trust. You may even end up turning your naysayer into one of your biggest advocates.

Optimizing your Blog for the Search Engines

Search engines love blogs. They are text based, which makes them very easy for search engines to "read" and categorize. Take a moment to use Google's free keyword research tool. You can find it under Google Adwords, Google.com/sktool/ or search "keyword tool" on Google. (The link to this resource keeps changing). Here you can enter keywords related to your industry and what services and ideas you hope to be found for online. The keyword tool will show you a list of related terms by competition (how many other web sites are competing for that same term) and search volume (how many people are actually searching for that term). You want to find the best keyword phrases that describe your business and services, and that have the highest search volume and lowest competition. Once you've identified these keywords, use them whenever you can as you set up your blog. You can even use them in your blog's name, URL and in the category (pages) within your blog.

When you write a new blog, you will also have the opportunity to include keywords as tags. Tags not only help Google and other search engines know more about what your blog post is about, but they are also used by the blog network to categorize your post and promote it. This is important because it helps the blog network identify which other blogs may be similar to your topic, and will promote your blog to that audience. For example, when you read a blog that was built with WordPress.com or Blogger.com, you will often see a list of 2-3 links to related posts at the end of the article you just read. These links are automatically selected based on keywords used in the article's tags as well as keywords used in its headline. This is why, crafting an attention grabbing headline, with keywords, is so important to gaining access in front of new audiences.

Promoting your Blog post on other Social Networks

Most blogs like WordPress.com offer a setting to automatically post your latest entry to your other social networks, such as to your Twitter or Facebook account. We advise against this. Although it saves time, each of your audiences on these social networks may be a little different; therefore crafting a slightly different headline and incentive to click is beneficial.

Use a URL shortening service like bit.ly or goo.gl to create short URL's that you can use for Twitter, LinkedIn and others. Another benefit to using these URL shorteners, is that they offer the ability to track which links received the most clicks. This provides you with added data you can use to improve your messaging. (More on tracking in Chapter 7)

Finally, always include a great photo with your blog post. If you don't have one on hand, you can purchase stock photos from web sites like BigStockPhoto.com for a few dollars. Professional photos not only make your blog look more credible, but also help to draw attention to when you promote it on other social networks like LinkedIn.com or Facebook. Posts with great photos, get more clicks.

Your blog is also a potential source for reporters and bloggers writing about your topic. Today's journalists use the Internet to research and find ideas for their next story. The comments and interest of fans, followers and friends help journalists get an indication of interest a particular story or topic will have. The more comments a topic has, the more likely the journalist will be to pursue that story. Therefore, optimizing your blog posts, and social networking updates for keywords is essential for coming up in a journalist's research path. However, if you'd rather not wait for the journalists to "find you", you can reach out to them. You can do this by determining the individual bloggers and journalists who may be interested in what you have to say and reaching out to each with a brief description of what you've written along with and why their readers would be interested. It's important to do the leg work of actually reading the writer's past articles so that you don't pitch a story on the latest energy saving strategies for the home to the publication's style editor. Most blogs and some online news media will include the writer's email address with their posts or in a Contact Us section.

Online publications and blogs need content, so like a relevant tweet, a good project or blog post can be picked up by influential players – amplifying and adding credibility to your message. Kenneth Caldwell, a San Francisco-based communications consultant for architecture and design firms, sends a customized pitch letter, a PDF of his clients' projects with images, and no more than one page of text to a targeted list of bloggers and journalists. "Online press and social media make it possible to get a story out in a few days, as opposed to six-to-12 months that it takes with print publications."

If you can't find a direct way to contact them through email, Twitter can be more effective in getting their attention. Search for the writer's name on Twitter and follow them. Then stay tuned. Listen to their tweets for an opening to contribute your own experience – then reply with something interesting. Once you have established a dialog with this person, you can suggest a story idea.

If your story warrants a broader appeal and you are looking for a way to broadcast your announcement to the social web, you may want to consider a hybrid of the traditional press release – the Social Media Release (SMR). The SMR is basically the evolution of the original that speaks more plainly to the intended reader and provides organized access to relevant information sources from across the web. Reporters, bloggers and anyone else who finds its content interesting can incorporate one or more elements of it into a blog post, status update or tweet. A typical SMR may include a list of facts relating to the announcement, supporting quotes, downloadable images and multimedia files, links related web pages as well as background information on the person or firm. (All keyword optimized, of course.) Ultimately an SMR is intended to appeal to traditional journalists as well as bloggers and consumers/readers. The big press release distribution services like PRWeb and BussinessWire can optimize your press release for social media, but there are a handful of free services, like PitchEngine, Pressitt and PRX that can do this as well. However, the mass customized distribution of these tools is the downside. "Social media is not about connecting with untold thousands, it's about using technology to find and connect with your very focused constituencies. It's still about relationships," reminds Caldwell.

Self-promotion on Facebook and LinkedIn

We are seeing more and more corporate executives and entrepreneurs use their Facebook profiles to promote themselves personally, outside of the more corporate company Facebook page. The idea is to "make your business personal". In other words, the more you share your personal side with readers and "friends" the stronger they will feel about your work. With that said, here are six ways to promote your personal profile page.

1. **Update your Facebook page frequently, but not more than 1x per day.**

   Each time you update your site, that information becomes available to all your friends via the News Feed feature. The New Feed feature even opens your information up to your friends' friends and is most successful at taking information viral. Stay away from posting mundane things like what you had for lunch, and instead post links, updates and information that are related to your brand and ideals. And always post your latest blog post. It's also a good idea to include a question to get your friends to comment and engage. Facebook posts that gain the most comments, stay at the top of the newsfeed longest, and get the most exposure.

2. **Upload photos**

   Photos help capture attention and according a 2012 survey by Dan Zarrella (http://danzarrella.com/infographic-how-to-get-more-likes-comments-and-shares-on-facebook.html#),, photos generate more likes and shares than posts including video, text only or links. Use colorful, casual, candid photos …it will help your profile stand out more in the news feeds as well as communicate a human element to your work. If you specialize in one area of your field, it's a good idea to post photos of yourself that help promote that brand. For example, a children's bookstore could post pictures of images from recent puppet show or author reading events.

3. **Tag Other Pages**

   Use the tagging feature to link to other companies or organizations related to your post. The pages you tag will be notified and are more likely to comment, like or share your post with their fans. This brings more attention to your profile and potential to link up with more fans. Seek out other industry "friends" where your services don't necessarily compete. Work together to build great ideas that you can share with both of your Facebook fan bases.

4. **Join Targeted Groups and Causes**

   Joining specific Facebook Groups and Causes that align with your thought-leadership mission (for example sustainability or green movements) opens you and your work up to more networks and potential "friends". Post something on the wall of that group that provides real value and gets conversations going. This will help draw attention to your own Facebook profile or page.

Ideas for Saving Time on Content Creation

The great thing about being a published author or public speaker is that you already have a wealth of information to pull from. You can edit excerpts from your book, articles and presentations and turn them into valuable blog posts. However, even this can be time consuming. Marcela Abadi Rhoads, author of the ADA Companion Guide, estimates she spends about 10 hours per week on social networking activities. She says she posts something every day and comments on something every day to help establish herself as an expert. Sometimes she will post original content, while other times she will post a link to a helpful article she found.

If you can manage it, participation on the social networks once a day is a great way to stay in the conversations. However you can also be quite effective with a once a week post – as long as that one post is of high quality and gets long lasting conversations going. Another strategy, which we recommend for our busy clients, is to spend 1-2 months posting many things, many times, on various social networks at various times of day. Then closely monitor the results so you can identify the absolute best times, places, and frequency to participate for maximum impact. We'll show you how to track all of these things in Chapter 7.

Another strategy for time-efficient participation is regular use of the social listening tools mentioned earlier in this chapter. Participate the moment you find a conversation happening online that you can contribute valuable insight to. This helps keep your social networking time spent extremely targeted.

"Although custom content creation is ideal for establishing yourself as a thought leader, doing so can be labor and time intensive. Fortunately, you don't always have to create every post from scratch. Save time by posting a link to an important article or industry trend and provide your own commentary."

Content sharing, or simply posting a link on your social networks to compelling information that someone else wrote is another easy way to generate fresh posts. Finding and sharing essential industry information can prove to consumers that your firm understand the industry, and has a genuine interest in wanting to help others in the industry keep informed on important trends. Plus, by posting a colleague's article to your social network, you are showing support of his/her ideas.

"Make your social profile the hub for all information centered around your subject expertise. Make it the first and final source potential clients and colleagues can come for information."

We are seeing more and more small business owners engage in content sharing activities as a way to generate fresh posts and establish themselves as an individual with a handle on the pulse of the industry. In fact, this strategy of content sharing is now being used by nearly half of all US marketing professionals; according to February 2011 research from the content curation firm HiveFire. More than 75% of those professionals engage in content curation for the primary purposes of establishing themselves as thought leaders and elevating brand visibility and buzz.

Ultimately, social media gives every person the chance to publish ideas and stand and scream from their own soap box, but the amount of information in circulation seems to be in an inverse proportion to our ability to pay attention. If thought leadership is your goal, you need to find a way to capture your readers attention – by doing something or saying something that is authentic and brave – but here's the catch, it has to be relevant.

Read the brief side bar on how one relevant tweet was retweeted more than 8000 times:

The Power of a Relevant Tweet

Scenario: On March 10, 2011 when the news about the magnitude 8.9 earthquake in Honshu, Japan broke, Dave Ewing (@DaveEwing) located in Colorado had been watching videos of Tokyo that showed a city holding its own again the fifth largest earthquake in history. Meanwhile, #prayforJapan was trending on Twitter.

He sent out a tweet. *The headline you won't be reading: "Millions saved in Japan by good engineering and government building codes". But it's the truth.*

What happened: According to Ewing's "A Bit Freaked Out" blog post, "The next morning I noticed my iPhone was awake. It was showing notifications of retweets — at what looked like about once a second. Yikes! When I checked my email, I had more than 300 new followers on twitter. Eeak!" A couple of hours later, his tweet was the top news item on Reddit, a website that ranks the popularity of what's currently happening online.

We saw the tweet as a retweet, but hadn't realized the expanse of its impact until we read about its success in a ClickZ.asia blog post by Vijay Sankaran. By searching for key words in the tweet on Topsy, a search engine for social media, we learned that Dave Ewing's tweet was forwarded more than 8,300 times. This was possible because more than 750 of those were by "influential" people, meaning their messages strongly influence the actions of others. This includes the more than 50,000 followers of Andy Carvin, who is a senior strategist at NPR and the more than 200,000 followers of Philip DeFranco, the host of The Phillip DeFranco Show Mondays through Fridays on his YouTube channel that has more than 1.7 million subscribers. Sankaran estimates that Dave Ewing's late night message may have reached millions of Twitter users across the world.

Equally influential in spreading Ewing's message are the well-read bloggers that were inspired by his tweet. San Francisco-area blogger Josh Rosenau who writes for ScienceBlogs used Ewing's tweet as his headline and opening statement in a post that analyzed the severity and destruction of the quake. U.K. online tabloid Anorak featured Ewing's tweet as an alternative perspective. "Japan Earthquake news headlines focus on the doom. But what about the wonder of humanity that created buildings able to withstand a tsunami? … What about thinking how much worse it would have been without human ingenuity?" A blogger in Amman, Jordan referenced the success of Ewing's tweet as the motivation for writing his post about earthquake preparedness. Prolific bloggers look for content ideas everywhere.

Why: At a time when people were looking for spiritual explanations and support, Dave Ewing drew the world's attention to the heroes of the crisis — engineers and building codes — all in 132 characters. By saying something different from everyone else, Ewing connected with people who were hungry for an optimistic point of view and eager to share it. (Although, he now wishes he'd said government *regulation* instead of *building codes*.)

Resources:

@DaveEwing

http://www.ewingdev.com/blog/

www.topsy.com

www.reddit.com

@acarvin

@PhillyD

www.youtube.com/sxephil#p

www.scienceblogs.com

www.anorak.co.uk

www.blog.ambitious.me

6
BUILDING AND NURTURING COMMUNITIES

By now, you should have narrowed in on your core business and marketing goals, identified your company's key influencers and/or potential thought leaders, and focused in on where and how your target audience engages online. For some of you, engaging in the various social networks is sufficient for achieving your objectives, but others may feel they need to do more than participate and engage. If this is you, now it's time to build your online community.

An Online Community is a place where like-minded individuals come together to share, learn, and exchange ideas with the use of Internet based tools. Therefore, your online community can live within any of the popular social networking sites such as a designated Twitter hash tag, a LinkedIn Group, Facebook page or as a sub-group within an already existing online community. You can also create and customize your own community outside these existing groups in the form of a blog, forum or message board. With today's web tools, you can even set up an entire social networking site for your business, without having to know any web programming (more about this later in the chapter).

When you understand your target audience, along with your overall goals for growing your community, you can identify which Internet tools provide the best solutions for creating your online community. In some cases, you may choose multiple online platforms to develop your community.

Whatever platform you decide to use to build your online community, the crucial element is this: your community must have a clear purpose that your target audience cares about. Don't try to create a purpose. Instead, build off a purpose that many people are already passionate about, and will want to talk about.

The National American Institute of Architects found unexpected success in building a loyal online community base when they launched a Twitter chat. Followers simply used hashtag #aiachat to join a range of conversations of interest to fellow architects including sustainability, green design, design's influence on K-12 education, client relationships, and more. AIA Chat began as a simple feature of National Architecture Week and quickly grew from there. Although the conversations were lead by AIA, anyone could join in the conversation.

"I was overwhelmed at the participation rate and level of interaction of the first AIA Chat on Twitter," explained Sybil Walker Barnes, Director of Social Media for The American Institute of Architects in an email to us. "We had nearly 100 commenters (98) take part in the initial chat (not counting those who simply watched)."

"More important," she continued "I received a lot of feedback requesting to continue the conversation. It almost seemed as if our members and followers were looking for a community or a way to connect on Twitter. I had a lot of fun with the chat; they didn't have to twist my arm to continue it. I enjoy seeing the interactions among users during the chats and camaraderie that is developing among some of them that wasn't apparent prior to the chats.

"Since the initial chat, AIA Chat has continued monthly on the first Wednesdays of the month at 2pm Eastern Standard Time on Twitter. Last fall we extended it from 60 minutes to a 90-minute chat, again based on feedback. Even at the end of 90 minutes, some even continue amongst themselves."

AIA Chat on Twitter is only one of the many social media channels The American Institute of Architects is using to connect with the subset of their members who were congregating in social forums online. They also use LinkedIn and FaceBook, as well as their own social site, KnowledgeNet. The idea is to use technology that your target audience feels most comfortable interacting with.

Key Benefits of Building an Online Community

By developing and managing an active online community around your company's core values and strengths, your business then becomes a leader in your chosen area, and your members become your key influencers helping to spread your brand's mission. Masco Cabinetry may sell most of its products directly to consumers, but the company recognizes the influence of product recommendations and project specifications from members of the design profession. Director of Architect Relations & Education Mark Johnson, FAIA, was hired to build a community of architects, interior designers, custom builders and remodelers — segments beyond the traditional "kitchen & bath" industry that Masco had never reached before.

Twitter is Johnson's network of choice. He does have a presence on Facebook and LinkedIn, but as Johnson explains, "Because of time constraints, the only way to develop content for multiple social media sites was to use a tool to aggregate, in my case Hootsuite." While he acknowledges that tweets can be "cryptic" on the other platforms, the 140 character limit makes Twitter the preferred platform for communicating and engaging quickly. "I've found that a relevant tweet to a relevant following can translate into significant click-throughs. With 3000 followers, I can drive 50-90 click throughs with a single tweet."

Managing an online community also gives you the opportunity to understand first hand what your target audience and/or industry needs based on member comments and interactions within the community. As a result, you can better position your business to develop solutions to core desires and problems. In the end, building an online community will help you to become a better company.

Building your own Social Networking site

We remember a time not too long ago when the cost to develop your own social networking site was upwards of half a million dollars in programming fees alone. Today, you can get a social networking site launched for as little as $19/month and you don't have to know a thing about programming. Web sites like Ning.com allow you to set up a full social networking site with all the core community features such as forums, blogs, and various widgets to help you reach your goals. You can even choose the colors and layout of your social network to match your firm's existing web site or marketing materials. Ning.com also provides an easy "single sign-on" option, which allows people to use their Facebook, Google or other social networking site login to join your community. Allowing members to use existing social profiles to login makes the barrier to entry even easier.

Forums or message boards are perhaps the oldest form of social networking and remain a core function of most online communities. Internet users participated in forums long before Facebook, MySpace or even blogs existed. And there is a reason they have survived. They are easy to use and they work. Forums give members an easy way to ask questions and share ideas. They also provide lots of great keyword-friendly text and links that search engines love. The more activity your forums have around a particular topic or industry question, the more likely you'll be to show up on the top of the search engines.

While there are several do-it-yourself forum options available, bigger firms hoping to grow a larger community may want to consider hiring a company such as Lithium (www.lithium.com). Lithium is a California based company that can help you customize a community forum that will also tie into popular social networks such as Twitter and FaceBook. An added benefit to hiring a full service company like Lithium (over a do-it-yourself service like Ning.com) is access to services like 24/7 moderation. Such a service can be an important time-saver if you don't have extra staff on-hand to regularly check into a fast growing community. We found that using a full service company like Lithium was critical while setting up Verizon's online community. Thousands of members and hundreds of posts were made within the online community on a daily basis. Outside moderators helped Verizon's internal staff identify both potential problems as well as influential members who could keep the community running.

While few small businesses will be able to generate a community as big and as active as Verizon's; the roles of moderator and community manger are vitally important and can be time consuming. Speaking about the amount of time he invested in building his community, Mark Johnson noted, "The first four months on Twitter, I averaged three-to-four hours per day, seven days a week — much of it on my own time. To continue growing a community and engaging followers takes at least an hour a day, better if I can devote two hours per day."

If you can't dedicate a resource to this we recommend that small businesses consider outsourcing moderation and/or a community manager role, so that the day-to-day management requirements doesn't prevent your online community form thriving.

Designating a Community Manager

In a perfect world, your community members would keep conversations buzzing and topics tasteful. However, in the real world, online communities don't run themselves. And if you want to keep your online community on track and consistently reflecting your company's missions, values and business goals, you need to designate a community manager.

The cost and type of moderation you need can vary depending on the size and nature of your community. Some companies can get away with tasking the job of moderator to an internal marketing person, however some companies choose to outsource this job. Companies like London-based eModeration boast $7 million in revenue to moderate large communities such as MTV, ESPN and the Economists. While you can easily find someone overseas to moderate your community for $5/hour (verses eModeration's $30-$40/hour), moderating today's communities is less about simply filtering dirty language, and more about engaging with members in a meaningful way that keeps your company's brand and goals in the forefront. It's critical that your moderators understand your business, products and your audience. In fact, this is the exact reason BabyCenter.com, one of the largest online communities for new moms, hired 10 "real mom" moderators that were recruited directly from the site's own message boards.

Whoever you designate, it must be someone who understands the reason you set up this community in the first place and will adhere to your company's social media guidelines (as discussed in chapter 4).

Community managers need to have the authority to take action (under set guidelines) should a heated online debate happen within your community in the middle of the night. Sometimes, a single negative post within your community that remains un-managed can spread like a virus, generating multiples of comments during the wee hours of the night. By the time you roll into the office the next morning, the damage is done. Having a designated community manager responsible for monitoring the community at all times is an important piece of controlling the direction of your community's voice.

Your community manger must also care about the growth of your community and its members. Knowledge Architecture created a community around its annual event, KA Connect. The community is nurtured by the firm Founder Chris Parsons and it is truly a labor love. Especially at the beginning, community managers, like Parsons, aren't just shepherding conversations by responding to posts and comments, they are privately encouraging members to post new topics and comments. It's the community manager's responsibility to facilitate content, dialogue and a positive atmosphere in the community that encourages members to participate. Read the KA Connect case study to find out what it takes to grow a highly engaged community:

Case Study

Firm: Knowledge Architecture (KA), San Francisco, California

Project: KA Connect

Challenge: Chris Parsons launched KA in 2009 with a software solution to help medium-to-large construction industry companies make the most of their data, knowledge and expertise. His frustration, as a former in-house IT leader, was that the discussions about knowledge management tended to focus on people talking about technology infrastructure. Parsons believed that in order for KA to be successful, he needed to move the conversation toward information and away from technology. If he were to be successful at selling knowledge management, he needed to expand his audience from the CIO and IT staff to include marketing and operations managers discussing these concepts.

With his company only four months old, Parsons announced to his LinkedIn connections that he was going to host an event called KA Connect to define "knowledge management" through applied examples. Then he built a website and a blog to help promote the event. The 2010 event was held in Chicago and featured a PechaKucha 20 x 20 format to start to define "knowledge management." Parsons lined up about 15 speakers of various disciplines and he expected 25-to-30 people to show up as attendees. To his surprise, more than 80 people came. The event did more than share success stories. The interactive format led to conversations, debates and new ideas. According to Parsons, "At the end of the event, it felt like we were just getting started."

Originating in Tokyo in 2003 by two young architects, PechaKucha networking events, or "20 x 20's" take place in many cities small and large around the world. The PechaKucha format is a short presentation of a singular idea, 20 slides that are automatically advanced every 20 seconds for a total presentation time of 6 minutes, 40 seconds. At the end of the 6 minutes 40 seconds another presenter takes the stage. The concise, fast-paced format allows ideas to be exchanged rapidly and opens up time and attention for discussion."

Objective: To capture the momentum started by the event and continue the conversations in a new forum.

Strategy: The day after the event, Parsons sent an email to all who attended the event and to those who expressed interest in attending but couldn't make it, to announce a new KA Connect Group on LinkedIn. Within days, members were posing questions — both practical and philosophical-to the group and getting thoughtful responses. This was not without effort on the part of Parsons though.

As manager of the group, Parsons is heavily involved. Parsons developed a three-step regimen, as shown in figure 6.2, that he follows each time he is introduced to someone or accepts their business card:

1. Add their name to the KA email marketing list.

2. Personally connect with them on LinkedIn.

3. Invite this person to join the KA Connect LinkedIn group.

Through his diligence in growing the community and through grass roots referrals from members, the group has grown steadily from that first day.

The KA Connect Group is a closed group, so people have to be accepted to the group to become a member. When Parsons receives a request to join, he sends a personalized welcome letter to each new member. While the same information is shared in each letter, he tailors the message to what he knows about this person. Parsons also uses this initial communication to get feedback from them by asking what they are interested in learning and how they found out about the group.

The KA Connect content is mostly contributed by others in the group but, as figure 6.3 depicts, Parsons' fingerprints are all over them. Every new discussion passes through him before it is posted and often Parsons will respond privately to the initiator with some minor editorial tweaks or suggestions to make the post more likely to ignite a response from other members before he approves it. Sometimes he is involved even before this. Parsons shared an example with us of a simple phone conversation with one of the 2011 KA Connect presenters during the lead-up to the event, "He asked for a suggestion about working within the 20 slides x 20 seconds format. So instead of telling him what I thought, I asked him to query the group." But Parsons doesn't stop there. He also actively solicits discussion. Parsons regularly emails KA Connect members when he sees a connection between their professional work/interests and a conversation thread to suggest that they contribute their point of view. He draws a line at editing comments so that these can be spontaneous and change course as conversations naturally do — with the exception of the very rare personal attacks, which he removes completely.

Parsons also uses the LinkedIn group to generate responses and/or start a new discussion about something that has been added to the KA Connect blog or website. For example, after the 2010 live KA Connect event, Parsons posted the videos of each presentation to the event's website and to iTunes. Periodically, he would start a new discussion that features a key point from one of the presentations, noting (and linking to) the recording and posing a related question to the group. On the KA Connect blog, guest blog entries often originate in the same way as the discussions threads — as a result of something someone said to Parsons in person, on the phone or in an email. Parsons stops them after they've made an interesting point and asks them to write a blog post on the topic and then follows up later to remind them that he is still interested.

Results: In July 2012 the KA Connect Group on LinkedIn amassed approximately 1,500 members. By our estimation, two-to-three new discussions are started each week. Almost all of these generate a few comments from group members, some generate upwards of 20 to 60 comments. Discussions sometimes stay active for months — thanks in part to LinkedIn's group digests and opt-in automated emails that notify you when someone replies to a discussion that you have commented on or liked.

There has also been a steady increase in number of attendees at the 2011 and 2012 KA Connect events.

Beyond the statistics, Parsons will tell you that the discussions that take place here are also helpful to his business. Points that are made here help him refine his perspective on these topics. The group is also a resource that he turns to with his own questions.

Lessons: Community and the degree of comfort needed in an environment where people openly share ideas and offer feedback, is something that KA works to create inside its client organizations. Parsons attributes much of the success of KA Connect to its in-person start. In fact, he often advises his clients to physically bring people together — even just once every couple of years — as a way of making internal communications tools more effective. While most of its members have not attended the KA Connect real world events, those who have attended are the most active in the forum. The result is a genuine feeling of camaraderie and willingness to help one another.

It's still about relationships. Find ways to bring your community together in the real world to breathe new life into your circle and to strengthen the connections between individuals.

Resources:

http://knowledge-architecture.com/

http://www.ka-connect.com/

http://www.linkedin.com/groups?home=&gid=2952414&trk=anet_ug_hm

http://twitter.com/karchitecture

http://www.facebook.com/pages/KA-Connect/114305828595366

The tools you use to build your community and how you choose to manage it are important considerations. However, even more vital to your community's success will be the influence of its core members.

Online Communities Need Loyal Members

The key ingredient to online community success is the passion and loyalty of its members. Without members, you have no followers, no fans, no key influencers, no one engaging with your ideas, and no one looking to you as a leader in your field, in other words, no community. That's why we have put this chapter near the end of the book. Nurturing and building an online community comes after you have a marketing plan in place to let potential followers know about the benefits of joining your community.

Building up a community may come quicker for those successful businesses who already have a strong offline following, especially for those companies who also have a well-known mission or brand tied to a strong social purpose or cause. These companies can further expand their industry influence by channeling ideas into an online community, where they can watch followers expand on ideas and help them flourish.

The San Diego Rescue Mission, a local nonprofit that provides meals, shelter and rehabilitation programs for the homeless, uses its Facebook page as the center piece of its online community. As the moderator of their Facebook page, we regularly share stories about the people who have been helped by The Mission. We also take time to publically thank individuals and companies who have donated time, materials or funds. Adding a photo of the volunteers and/or tagging the companies involved, helps gain attention and increases the likihood of those volunteers sharing the message again with their Facebook fans and friends.

Leveraging "real world" relationships to build momentum in your online community is certainly Mark Johnson's strategy. At the time of this writing, Johnson is developing a design blog on the Masco Cabinetry website which will be launched in the coming weeks. "Hopefully, my existing followers will build a blog following much faster than starting from scratch," explained Johnson.

However, with today's cost-effective social tools and viral nature of the web, even an individual, a smaller, or less known company can develop a loyal online community following. Johnson suggests becoming a content aggregator. "You can't be an expert in everything, and the experts appreciate you pointing others to their content to help build their following." Johnson publishes 25 to 30 e-newspapers on topics ranging from 3D rendering to social media five days a week. "I'm aggregating the expert content from many others into a single topic e-newspaper which is probably faster than users doing web searches on their own."

Whether you are a large, well-know company, or a smaller consultancy, the following list of action items can encourage membership in your online community.

1. **Invite Members to Join.**

   When you are ready to launch your new online community, personally invite contacts who would contribute or benefit form the community. Send a personal email inviting your close contacts to be among the first members. This will give you a chance to get honest feedback on content you've populated the community with, as well as generate membership, comments and activity before you announce your community to the world.

   Make your first members feel important. Introduce them to each other. Seed valuable content and give new members clear actions to take. For example, ask for their feedback on a specific blog post or forum topic. By making them feel a part of the community, they are more likely to contribute and recommend it to their peers.

2. **Announce your Community to your Target Audience**

   In Chapter 2, we discussed ways to find your target audience. As you join and listen in on existing groups your audience is participating, take time to make insightful and valuable comments or offer solutions to problems or questions. Then at the end of your comment, let members know that your firm recently started a community around this exact topic, and offer the direct link if they'd like to join.

3. **Let Members know how they can contribute to the Community.**

An often overlooked, but powerful tool for encouraging engagement of new members is the Welcome Email. Depending on what tool you use to build your online community, you can set up an automatic "welcome email" that thanks members for joining and confirms their registration with your community. While most community mangers leave the welcome email at that, you can benefit from taking this email a step further. After all, this welcome email is your first engagement with a new member. It's a critical point when the member will decide whether or not they want to become more active in your community.

In your welcome email, provide links to your best content areas and active discussions. As your community evolves, so will your welcome email. It's also beneficial to provide new members with a direct link where they can introduce themselves and either ask a question or make a comment about why they joined. Sometimes, entering a close-knit community of industry professionals and peers can feel intimidating to the new member. You want to encourage them to introduce themselves to the group and become part of the conversation.

4. **Center your community on the members, not your company.**

It's all about the soft-sell here. You never want to use your community to push your business. Rather use it as a tool to build relationships with your target audiences and position your company as a leader in the industry. If members want to know exact services you provide or contact someone in sales, they can easily find your web site. Your community should focus on providing genuine, valuable content that matters to your members (and that reflects your company's overall marketing and business goals). The sales will follow.

Another way to make your community feel member-centered is to acknowledge and refer to influential members often. Consider interviewing members and incorporating their feedback into a weekly blog post. The more you show that you value your community member's input, the more likely they will be to continue to participate.

5. Take time to reward and build personal relationships with your top members

"Community Leaders" is a term used to describe the most active and influential members of an online community. Many times, these community leaders will end up gaining more respect and authority within a community than the person who built the online community to begin with. Therefore, it is essential that you build relationships with these powerful members. While a happy community leader can become one of your company's most powerful online advocates, an unhappy community leader can do a lot of damage to your brand.

Rewarding community leaders for their participation and contribution to your community is a great way to show your appreciation and encourage them to continue to engage. Rewarding members does not necessarily mean giving them free stuff. You can reward community leaders by simply recognizing them and acknowledging their contributions. You can also make them feel special by inviting them to participate in smaller groups of discussion or be the first to comment on a new project. For example, take the top 5-10 members in your community and let them be the first to learn about a new project you are working on, and seek feedback.

Another way you can reward community leaders is to recognize that they have lives outside of your community. Reward influential members by interviewing them and highlighting their work as it relates to your community's mission in your next blog post. Be sure to promote that member's blog/twitter account and/or company web site to show support for their business goals in return for helping yours.

Depending on the platform you've chosen to build your online community on, you may have the ability to offer members special titles, avatars, badges or icons to reflect their particular involvement in the community. While working with Verizon, we had several levels of titles and avatars members could use to show their involvement. With each level of participation, came added privileges, such as access to private message boards. Our most loyal and influential members received the Community Leader title and badge. This title was reserved for the select few based on how often they posted, as well as the value of those contributions. In order to keep conversations fresh, we selected a new group of community leaders every 6 months. We found that once we awarded members with such titles and special privileges, their positive participation grew and helped the community flourish. These community leaders were the first ones to step in and support the company on a heated debate or assist on a technical problem a customer was having. Sharing community "power" with your top members makes more people feel as if they have a vested interest in the success and growth of your company. Therefore, they are more likely to promote, defend and help your community thrive.

6. Build buzz and excitement with Appropriate Give-Aways

Melissa Caughey runs TillysNest.com, a popular blog among urban chicken enthusiasts. In addition to her engaging blog posts and memorable photos, she regularly rewards her loyal readers by giving away backyard chicken products sold by other companies competing for the same audience. By teaming with the other chicken web sites and offering to give-away their product, she not only gains access to more potential readers, but keeps her existing ones loyal.

"One way to drive business to your website or social media site is through the use of giveaways and contests." Caughey recommends "Whether your item is as large in size and value as a chicken coop or if it is as small as a book, people love the thrill of winning something for free. Contest rules can involve simply leaving a name or email address on my blog or be more complicated by participating in a few steps to increase their chances of winning" such as checking out the Facebook page of the company who's product she is giving away.

Product give-aways are great for generating community buzz and excitement, but use them in moderation. "In addition to the giveaways, it is important to keep top quality information on your website. Quality always prevails over quantity," she advises. "Finally, don't forget to share links to companies that you enjoy working with and forming partnerships that can help both of you reap the rewards at the same time."

Please note that if you plan to hold a contest or give away through a Facebook Community, important rules apply.

Top 4 Most Commonly Broken Facebook Rules

Many businesses choose to use Facebook as the platform for their online community. However, take note, that if you decide to use Facebook, you must adhere to their terms and conditions. Broken rules can result in having your entire Facebook page shut down, and all of your fans removed. Trust us! This has happened to many well-meaning businesses, who just forgot to follow these important rules.

1. If you are a business, you must use a Facebook Page — not a personal profile.

2. Your Facebook photo page cannot be an advertisement

3. Your Facebook photo cannot contain your web site address, phone number or other contact info

4. You cannot use Facebook features and functionality to run a contest. For example, you can't say "Like" or "Share" this post to win. And you can't use the "like" button as a way of voting. If you want to run a contest, you need to use a Facebook contest app. We like Wildfire (www.wildfireapp.com/) and North Social (www.northsocial.com), however there are plenty of free apps to choose from as well.

1. Be flexible about conversations and topics.

Social media is about what is happening now, and if current events or a new trend in the industry happens, you want your community to be flexible enough to become the centerpiece of conversation around it. Being the "go to" spot for your area of expertise is what makes your company a true leader in your field.

Listen to your community and let your community expand in a way that will encourage them to continue to contribute and share your company's values. This often involves having the courage to let go of control of the content of your community. Let members post blog entries or start topics in your forum. Although your social media strategy needs a clear direction, goals and plan, you need to stay flexible. True social media marketing includes the ability to be relevant, flexible and useful while developing a connection to your audience.

2. Let debates happen

Heated debates are an important (and fun!) element of community. Members wouldn't be there if they didn't feel passionate about your topic. Let debates happen and watch them unfold among members. If debates aren't happening, identify controversial topics around your community's core mission and plant the seed. Lively conversations that encourage active participation by many members is vital to the success and longevity of your community.

Sometimes a controversial topic will pop up around your company or a project you are working on. Nobody likes to see negative posts about themselves -especially within their own community. Resist the urge to delete. After all, a negative post shows that this is a genuine community, where people can truly say how they feel. It also keeps your target audience talking within YOUR community, rather than going else where to criticize your company or latest project. Keeping the unhappy member within your community gives you a chance to state your side of the story, and win them back. Take time to address any negative comments or concerns and if appropriate solicit member feedback on how you can fix the problem. If however, the negative comment is more of a rant, than constructive criticism, skip down to the next section to learn how you to handle such nasty posts.

3. Take the opportunity to meet up in person.

It's great to get to know people online, but when you have the chance meet people in real life. If many of your members are going to be at a conference or event, encourage or organize a meet up. Get to know people beyond the topic of your community and you may find more things you have in common. Mark Johnson has organized well attended "TweetUps" with his network at the National AIA conference and at the Kitchen and Bath Industry Show. Chris Parsons' community was born from an in-person event and community members organize local get-togethers through the LinkedIn Group. The better acquainted people are with each other the more willing they are to share their own experiences and offer input.

4. Protect your members (and yourself) from Trolls

In the world of online communities, trolls are those people who exist merely to leave negative comments on your blog, message boards or any place else you allow them to sneer. Trolls are not customers with a serious grievance or industry experts providing constructive criticism. They are internet users who literally troll social sites and add negativity and rants that can not only make a community owner's heart sink, but can also intimidate, influence and affect every member of a community. It is the community manager's job to identify and handle these trolls so they don't overrun your community.

A typical first reaction to a troll bad-mouthing your company, staff or a project you recently completed, will be to delete the negative comment. Avoid deleting at all costs. Once you start deleting posts, your community starts sounding more like a PR statement and less like a genuine community where all ideas are shared. Keep in mind that in some cases you should delete the post. Such cases include blatant spam, use of derogatory language, threats or harassment of other members of your community. In these cases, deletion and even banning the troll from the community is typically justified.

However, if it does not justify deletion or banning, how do you react to a troll comment? First, take a deep breath and never respond emotionally or by attacking the member back. This will only fuel the criticism and get others charged up to join the battle. Instead, show you are listening and that you appreciate them taking the time to express their concern. In other words, "kill them with kindness". Your best case scenario is that some of your loyal community members will jump to your defense and quiet the troll. And yes, it is acceptable to privately email your community leaders and encourage them to post a response to the negative comment.

The fact is that despite their nasty and loud voices, most trolls are quite insecure. And we have learned first hand that when enough community members post positive things contradicting what the troll said, they will back down. We've also seen a troll back off merely by the public reply from an official representative of the firm that was under attack... especially when the accusations made by the troll were exaggerated or false to begin with. Showing trolls that you not only have support, but are listening and will publicly react to their comments can be enough to quench false accusations or pointless rants.

Overall, your best strategy to keep the trolls away? Support your loyal members and encourage them to speak out and defend your company. Chances are, they will say all the things you wish you could say.

5. **Lack of participation in your community**

So you've built a great community and populated it with though-provoking content. You've also reached out to your contacts and invited them to join. Why aren't you getting more comments and participation? One reason may be that you don't have enough traffic to begin with. You need a fair amount of traffic coming to your online community to warrant conversations. Especially since only 10% of a community's overall traffic can be expected to posts anything. Most members prefer to merely watch and listen. What's more, of that 10% that will post something, only 1% will actually start a conversation. The other 9% will simply comment on other people's topics. This means that until you generate enough traffic to get conversations going, you will need to actively spark dialogue by posting questions and comments. In other words, members won't talk or contribute unless they see others doing so. So get some messages posted to encourage others to start talking.

One way to make your community appear more active is to grow it slowly. For example, don't start a community with too many different conversation topics or categories. It's better to have a few very active topics, then too many with too few conversations. Start with broad topics and see where the conversations go. You should naturally be able to identify which additional categories or message board topics should be added.

If your site appears too complicated and unfocused, people will not contribute. Having too much information can be intimidating to the first time member and can keep users from participating. Keep a feel of the pulse of your community by monitoring what topics are of most interest to them and expand areas and grow accordingly.

One final note on why you may not be getting contributions in your community. Members may simply think it's boring. Perhaps you've centered content too much around your company and not enough around what the members want or are interested in. Your community rules and guidelines may also be too strict. Meaning, you are moderating and editing comments too much and not letting passion and personality shine through.

Remember, that your community must be based on a topic that your target audience is passionate about. And passionate people want to be able to express themselves. If they feel their comments are getting filtered or your community is too controlled, they will go elsewhere. Build a community that lets your target audience share ideas and converse passionately, and watch your online reputation thrive.

7
EVALUATION STRATEGIES

You have deadlines to meet, projects to launch and new clients to pitch. You don't have time to devote endless hours to a social media plan that won't work. And you didn't dive into social media to win a popularity contest or to drive millions of viewers to your web site. You are building a social media campaign around your company's specific business and marketing goals, which you defined early on while reading this book. It is the cost and time it takes you to attain these goals that will measure the success of your social media efforts.

Unlike tracking traditional online marketing activities such as sending email newsletters, analyzing ad buys and monitoring web site traffic, social media campaign measurement can be a bit more elusive, because its not just about views, clicks and conversions.

Most digital metrics center around the beginning and end of the online relationships process. In other words, the first moment someone visits your web site (view, click), and then the final act of becoming a lead (frequency of conversion). Social Media falls somewhere in the center of this process and can be measured by engagement and interaction. When nurtured and implemented correctly, the strength of that engagement and quality of interaction will help a potential client (or journalist) form their ultimate decision about your company. It is these ongoing social interactions that help your connections ultimately decide whether they want to do business with you one time, multiple times, or, in a best case scenario, become an online advocate for you and your business.

Social media measurement therefore, goes well beyond the first or even final click. It encompasses how groups of people are engaging with you, your firm and/or your employee thought leaders within social networks, and if those interactions are helping you reach your ultimate goal.

"Social media click-counting is for people trying to impress their bosses or hold onto their jobs," explains Scott Doyon, Principal and Director of Marketing at PlaceMakers, LLC. "Its not that I'm against the value of benchmarks and measuring, and it does help us understand where we're getting traction among our topics and initiatives, but our greatest focus is on the relationships we're developing and the evaluation of which ones emerge from and transcended the looser realm of social media, where there's little expectation of meaningful commitment, to become solid business opportunities."

PlaceMakers' goal for social media is to create meaningful, lasting relationships with people that may eventually become their client, business partner or valued media connection. It is not about how many unknown Twitter followers they can collect or even attracting massive visitors to comment on their most recent blog post. It's about the quality of engagement they receive as a result of their participation in the social networks. It's about building real relationships that will lead to real opportunities.

Defining the Health of Your Online Community

Lithium Technologies, a firm that develops social media technologies and online communities for corporations, developed a way to predict success of a growing social network. They call this measurement the "Community Health Index". This report goes beyond the number of visits a community receives, but calculates the health of an online community by how well it meets the expectations and needs of the members.

Key attributes of a healthy, and therefore successful, community include growth (increasing membership), usefulness (great, relevant content), popularity (overall importance in your industry), responsiveness (how quickly members respond to questions and posts), interactivity (how many members contribute at all) and liveliness (positive buzz and vibrancy a community and its members exude).

At first glance, basing your measurement of community success on the happiness of your members can seem irrespective of your overall business goals. However, remember that social media success is not just about one-time clicks and a quick sale. Building a lasting and useful social media presence takes time and patience. And building up a network where your target audience is happy and continues to participate, will eventually help with your overall return of investment in your social media efforts.

The healthier your community becomes, the more likely your target audience will start to engage on your behalf and the less time you need to find members, develop new content and get conversations going. When members start volunteering to help you out by posting thoughtful, relevant content and recruiting new members themselves, it helps your bottom line in the fact that you can maintain a powerful social presence without necessarily having to be in the conversations every day. With that said, you'll still need a listening tool, to keep track of what is being said about your company.

Tracking Social Listening

A powerful, yet often overlooked benefit of social media marketing is the ability to listen to conversations related to your business goals. There are many different levels and costs associated with listening tools. The most basic, and free, is Google Alerts. Google alerts works well for smaller companies without a huge web presence, and offers a basic level of social listening. Simply go to GoogleAlerts.com, provide your email address and some core keyword phrases (including your company name and the names of your employee/company thought-leaders) and you will get an email alert each time these topics appear on the web. This will allow you to listen in, and see what is being said about your people and your firm online — and can also be a good way to keep track of competitors.

For larger companies however, that are aggressively taking on social media, I suggest using a professional social listening tool such as Radian6 (Radian6.com). A Radian6 tool goes beyond a Google Alerts by providing deeper analysis of conversations happening online.

A tool like Radian6 essentially helps you cut through the noise of social media and zero in on influential people talking about your company. This is ideal for busy professionals and firms that get a lot of media attention, because rather than having to read through every Google Alert that comes in, you can let the Radian6 dashboard advise you on which posts are most critical for you to respond to based on how much influence the person who posted the comment about your firm, has. Finally, you can get a feel for the overall sentiment of internet users in regard to your company, projects and industry and even look at comparisons on how your company compares to your competitors.

Think of social media as the world's biggest focus group. By using listening tools you can discover what your target audience wants. This information can then be incorporated into your overall marketing strategy and help you reach your goals.

While the above examples can help you monitor the overall health of your networks and listen to what is being said about your company, there are also many tools that let you track specific activities within your social networks, such as how friends and followers are reacting to your latest tweet or Facebook post. In these cases clicks and views can be important in helping you determine what types of content, as well as frequency, is of most interest to your audience, so that you can take steps to build community health.

Many professionals are tracking their social media efforts are using a combination of tracking tools such as Hootsuite and Google Analytics.

"Even with its free level, Hootsuite offers so much for the user," said Deborah Reale, Marketing Specialist of Reed Construction Data, who uses the Hootsuite dashboard to monitor several social networking channels simultaneously, including Twitter, FaceBook and LinkedIn. "Hootsuite gives analytics, which helps me identify our influencers."

Nick Bryan, Public Relations Manager for HMC Architects, uses a combination of several tracking tools including Google Analytics, Hootsuite and Chartbeat to monitor the success of their social media efforts. "Hootsuite overlays HMC tweets with our web site and blog traffic, thus connecting our tweets with web site hits" he explains. Chartbeat is a subscription-based tool that shows you what is happening on your website or blog at that moment. "We are able to tell which tweets were popular and where users browsed to after their initial click. Using Chartbeat to understand which pages on the web site are most popular, gives our PR team insight as to which content is critical to keep fresh and updated."

Mark Johnson of Masco Cabinetry checks on his Twitter progress with Hootsuite to unfollowing people who haven't tweeted in a month or more and to test the number of click-throughs per tweet. He also checks out his Klout score and the scores of a few Twitter mentors to compare.

Google Analytics

Although there are plenty of robust (and expensive!) web analytics tools available, Google Analytics is an essential one that any business engaging in new media marketing must use. It's free, easy to set up, and provides valuable information about your web site's activity. Although Google Analytics will not show you the health and engagement of your social media efforts, it will show you what people who come from these social media channels eventually do when they finally visit your web site. For example, do your Twitter followers fill out your "contact us" form and become quality leads? Do Facebook friends check out the most pages of your online portfolio? Getting a sense for which online community drives the most desirable traffic to your site will help you determine which social network to invest more time to reach your overall business and marketing goals.

When Lake Flato, a Texas based Architecture firm, approached us to help them develop a social media marketing strategy, one of the first things we did was set up Google Analytics. By analyzing their current web site's activity, we could quickly gauge which type of projects were of most interest to current web site visitors. This data can be used to help generate ideas of what topics can become the basis of content for the campaign.

Another important item we looked at was the bounce rate. In other words, when people got to the Lake Flato web site, were they engaging with it, or simply leaving (bouncing) without visiting any other pages? Google Analytics showed us that in fact the Lake Flato web site was engaging and therefore ready to capture the leads a well-considered social media strategy could deliver to the site. Work with an online marketing consultant and web developer to ensure your web sites bounce rate is around 30%. A bounce rate at above 50% means you are loosing more than half of your traffic, and your web site may not yet be ready for social media campaign.

Google Analytics also provided insight into the keywords people were using on the search engines to find the Lake Flato web site. From the keyword report, we discovered that more than 75% of Lake Flato's traffic was coming from people who already knew the company name.

This shows strong name brand recognition, and successful traditional PR and offline marketing efforts. However it also showed that they were missing a large portion of un-branded search terms which meant they were missing out on a significant amount of traffic from people searching for high quality, sustainable architecture services, but were not necessarily familiar with, or thinking about the Lake Flato brand during their online research. These un-branded keyword phrases therefore, can be used as the centerpiece of a social media campaign to help drive additional search traffic from potential customers looking for architecture services.

Google offers a variety of free keyword tools, to help you discover the best keyword phrases to optimize your web site and social media campaign. Type in words related to your service and Google will pull up a list of related phrases. For best result, look for a few top phrases that offer a high search volume with low competition. WordTracker. com and MarketSamurai.com are also great keyword discovery tools, and have a small monthly fee associated after your free trial expires.

Another way to really narrow in on best keyword phrases to use throughout your social media efforts is to set up a Google AdWords campaign. This will allow you to not only see which keywords deliver the most quality traffic to your web site, but which keyword phrases actually convert to quality leads.

Measuring Search Engine Optimization

Engagement is not only key to building lasting relationships with your online connections, but will also help increase your search engine ranking and exposure online. Google's algorithms were recently updated to give companies with the most "social authority" more weight in the search engines. Social authority is not only measured by how many friends, followers or fans you have, but also by how much engagement each of your posts receives. For example a Facebook post that receives several comments and likes, a tweet that gets "re-tweeted" and a blog post that receives many link backs and comments are all ways Google measures how much authority you have on the social web. Combining these great comments, tweets and posts with your core keyword phrases will help your web site, blog and social profile show up in the research path of your next potential client looking for your services.

This increase in search ranking is one of the core outcomes that HPD Architecture is hoping for through their social media campaigns.

"We are measuring the effectiveness of our social media campaign by increased unique visits to our web site, increased personal referrals for prospective clients or projects leads, and improvement of where our online listing(s) appear in the search engines (ie, first page of Google) associated with specific keyword searches," explains Laura Davis, Vice President and Director of Marketing for HPD Architects.

Tracking through URL Shorteners

URL shorteners provide an easy way to make those ugly blog URLs and long company landing page web site addresses appear cleaner and more concise. They are also essential for use in Twitter, where tweets need to be kept to 140 characters or less. There are hundreds of URL shortener services available. We recommend you use one that will also help you track activity. When you sign up for an account, Bit.ly and Goo.gl both provide useful stats on click activity. And better yet, these two sites are recognized by Google's search algorithm as trusted sources. This means that using them to shorten your URL will help your link building efforts as they relate to your search engine optimization strategy.

Facebook Insights

Facebook Insights in the analytics program associated with your firms Facebook page. While Google Analytics can merely show you that traffic came to your web site as a result of Facebook, the Facebook Insights will show you what posts actually generated the most engagement with your firm. You can view the interactions each of your posts has, and even review the time of day you made the post, so you can get a feel for best time to post moving forward based on your audiences usage habit.

WordPress and YouTube also have their versions of in-page analytics so you can monitor how people react to your content. As we write this book, Twitter and LinkedIn are releasing their versions of analytics as well.

The most exciting thing about social media is that it happens in real time. Which means you can test multiple types of messaging and gain instant feedback on what works and what doesn't. Try different hash tags, and industry questions on Twitter. Post a hot topic or surprising industry fact on Facebook. Then use multiple analytic tools to monitor and track the interactions to determine engagement, interest, health and ultimately, to discover which activities lead to completing your business goals in the most time efficient and cost effective way. Using tracking tools will help you understand quickly what resonates with your audience and encourages them to share your information on other networks. With that said, it's important to note that just because one particular comment works to generate leads one week, does not automatically mean it will generate the same results the next. Social media involves real people and real interactions, which means outcomes are not always predictable, even with the most sophisticated tools. However, the tools available will help you build healthier, more engaging networks in the long term, and in the end, help you cut through the noise and attain a better ROI for your social media campaign goals. Just like building relationships in real life, social media marketing it's not an overnight process; it's a long term commitment.

Arthur Nielsen once said, "The price of light is less than the cost of darkness". Quite simply, taking time to invest in social media analytics and understanding what your target audience wants is invaluable. Strategic and thoughtful ongoing listening and analysis of the social web is critical. Patience and timing are key. Understanding digital analytics and social media measurements and how that data impacts your business goals will provide you with the ability to make better decisions and become more accountable for your company's actions. And in the end, active social media monitoring will turn your firm into a better and more profitable company.

8
THE FUTURE OF SOCIAL MEDIA

As we write this book, updates and new tools are being added to Facebook, LinkedIn, Twitter, YouTube and Google+. We are seeing hot new social web sites like the virtual pinboard Pinterest emerge, and there is sure to be more by the time this book reaches your hands. Rather than try to share the latest nuance of each social network with you, this book is designed to give you the big-picture of how you can use social media (whichever tool and site you decide to use) to enhance your business. By understanding social media and implementing the best practices in this book, your company will be ready to adapt and flourish as the world of social media gets more and more integrated into our daily lives.

Step outside and you'll see that the digital world is already spilling out of our computer screens and quickly weaving itself into our daily, physical lives. According to a 2012 research survey by Forrester, more than 1 billion people will have a smartphone by 2016. This allows immediate access to the social web anytime, anywhere. And as smartphones continue to evolve into multi-functional devices they will take over tasks that used to require other objects. Some predict that these sleek handheld mobile devices will eventually replace such essentials as your wallet and keys and become a natural way of engaging with the physical world around us.

You have probably seen Quick Response (QR) codes on packaging and products in stores. QR codes are black and white boxes that look like bar codes and that function similar to radio frequency identification (RFID) tags. You see QR codes in more and more places — on the pages of print magazines or on outdoor billboards, for example. You can get a QR reader application on your smartphone, like the free ScanLife or any of the dozens of other free or paid versions, and then scan the QR code (or regular barcode) and gain additional information such as a coupon or even opt into a contest.

As the QR code's popularity grows, so does its size. To promote a dinosaur exhibit, a person-sized QR code was displayed on one of the walls of Madison Square Garden in New York, N.Y. Passersby scanned the enormous code using a QR code reader application on their mobile phone for the opportunity to upload their "biggest dinosaur roar" in a contest. Anyone who entered a roar had a chance to win tickets to the popular Walking with Dinosaurs show at Madison Square Garden.

We are also seeing more subtle uses of QR codes in our physical world. Realtors are embedding QR codes on "For Sale" signs and buildings. By scanning the QR code, interested buyers can view floorplans, prices and even videos of a building immediately on their smartphones as they stand near the sign.

In the future, we could see QR codes as common features on signage for famous landmarks or city buildings. Visitors could easily scan the code to know more about the creation of the building or the products and services inside.

As more people use smartphones to engage with the physical world in a networked way, they will begin to leave more and more digital breadcrumbs about where they have been, what they like and how they behave on a daily basis. City and state governments are already recognizing the power of these tools for interacting with constituents — and the power of the data that this creates.

Growth of Location-Based Social Networking

In case you are not familiar with location-based social networks like Foursquare, it is a web site that allows you to "check in" via your GPS-enabled mobile devices such as your smartphone or iPad. Once you check in, you can see if any of your friends or coworkers have checked in to nearby venues. You can also gain rewards for checking in at specific locations. For example, if the location owner has "claimed the venue" and is using Foursquare as a marketing channel, you may get a special message or unlock a secret coupon. Foursquare also doubles as a social game. People try to check in to as many places as possible to earn badges and become the virtual "mayor" of a specific place. In some cases, becoming a mayor or having certain badges will earn them discounts and coupons, in other cases, it is simply a contest in order to online recognition for having the most check ins at a particular place. This idea of check ins is gaining momentum. According to the Foursquare blog, the site grew 3,400% from 2009 — 2010, with the 6 millionth user signing up in January 2011.

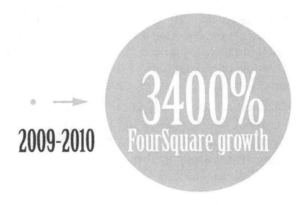

Figure 8.1: Foursquare's rapid growth.

Another location-based tool is the referral site Yelp. With more than 27 million reviews-mostly on restaurants, shops and nightlife-and millions of visitors to the site each day, local businesses can't ignore the power of this network because whether you, as a business-owner, choose to engage Yelp or not, it's very likely your customers already are. It's free for businesses to set up a page on Yelp and add descriptions, photos and even information about current promotions or special offers. Yelp also offers plenty of ways business can pay to enhance a listing further. Options are available to raise your chances of showing up in a potential customer's search path with Yelp's pay-per-click service or by offering a Yelp Deal.

Yelp is more than just a forum for reviews, it can also help owners and managers monitor public perception and fine tune their product and service offerings. A 2011 study (PDF) from Harvard Business School (http://www.hbs.edu/research/pdf/12-016.pdf) indicates that restaurants that improve their Yelp ranking by one full star could see increases in revenue from 5% to 9%. Businesses can also join the conversation by communicating publicly with all your readers or privately responding to individual reviewers — giving you the opportunity to address any negative experiences directly.

The Reputation Economy Is Coming

"The reputation economy is an environment where brands are built based on how they are perceived online and the promise they deliver offline," Dan Schawbel wrote in his February 2011 "Personal Branding" blog http://blogs.forbes.com/danschawbel/2011/02/21/5-reasons-why-your-online-presence-will-replace-your-resume-in-10-years/ for Forbes. Schawbel predicts that your online reputation will surpass your paper resume. "I believe that in order to compete in the global economy, you have to have an online personal brand. After you create that presence, you have to maintain it throughout the course of your entire life, before someone else does it for you."

Most employers already understand the impact of an online reputation. According to a January 2011 Microsoft Survey http://www.microsoft.com/privacy/dpd/default.aspx, 80% of hiring managers use online reputation information in their hiring process and 70% said they rejected candidates due to information they discovered about them online.

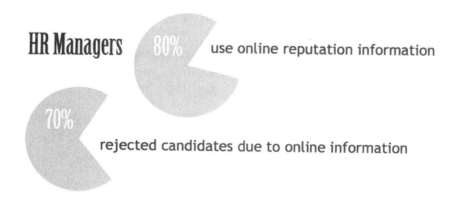

HR Managers 80% use online reputation information

70% rejected candidates due to online information

Figure 8.2: Microsoft Survey of how hiring managers use online reputation information.

More companies are realizing the value employees with a great online reputation can bring to a business. Salesforce's CEO Mark Benioff told Forbes Editor Victoria Barret in an onstage interview at a GigaOM's Net:Work conference about his idea of using technologies to gauge an employee's online reputation and influence to increase an employee's pay. During the interview, he suggested that employees who make an impact with online contributions should be rewarded with extra bonuses.

A new online social game called Empire Avenue empireavenue.com allows you to take stock in the future value of online influencers. The social network functions like a stock exchange where you can buy and sell shares of other members' profiles using virtual currency called "eaves." The value of a person's profile increases the more they participate in social networks. Although currently only an online game for fake money, you can see where this trend is heading. Online influence is valuable. And predicting the future online influence of employees and coworkers is even more valuable.

Until real money is at stake, this is an interesting way to get an understanding of the influence and value of some members of specific industries and what trends lead to buying and selling stock in thought leaders.

The Critical Role of Influencers In Your Social Media Strategy

As more and more people engage in social media, we predict they will rely more heavily on the recommendations of primary influencers or thought leaders to help them sort through the millions of messages and separate the noise from information that is relevant to their particular lives.

Technology companies are already seeing the need for firms to find and gain access to such influential social media users. Currently each company offers different algorithms to predict and identify "influence" over a particular group. These tools provide insight beyond how many followers or friends a person may have but calculate influence by how many people retweet or comment on that person's post. Some websites worth watching include Klout klout.com/home and MPact www.mpact.com. Klout, which received $8.5 million in new funding in early 2011, is an application that measures a person's online influence by reach, amplification probability and network influence. MPact is a similar application but allows you to find influencers by specific keywords or industry.

Big brands are already jumping on this data. Disney used Klout to identify 500 influential online moms. Once identified, Disney sent the moms passes to a free screening of the new movie Tangled and mailed their children a kit of Tangled merchandise. Leapster, an educational learning system designed by Emeryville, California-based LeapFrog Enterprises www.leapfrog.com, identified top influential parents in the social space and now pays them to write regular blogs. Luxury hotels in Vegas are using similar data to offer special incentives and preferential treatment to customers with the biggest social influence.

As you build your marketing plans for the architecture and building industry, consider using these tools to discover who your most influential customers are and how you can encourage them to talk about your brand in a positive way with their followers.

How Social Media Will Impact Journalism

With the explosion of blogs, we have already seen how the everyday person can impact journalism and even compete with recognized, long-standing traditional news media. However, as more and more companies get on board with social media in a strategic way, we expect to see more "citizen journalism" and "brand journalism," where thoughts and ideas are shaped by industry leaders and online advocates. Social media marketers already have a name for fans who spread a company's values and thoughts: brand evangelists.

Further Customization of Social Networks and Tools

As more and more companies use Facebook, we predict we will see a growing need for additional widgets and customization tools to make Facebook pages do more. From free Facebook apps to paid monthly services like North Social: www.northsocial.com, we will see more and more companies begin to customize their Facebook pages to engage in more powerful ways with customers and fans.

In 2011, Facebook announced the average media site that integrated a Facebook like button or other Facebook plugin saw a 300% increase in referral traffic: http://searchengineland.com/by-the-numbers-how-facebook-says-likes-social-plugins-help-websites-76061.

And the type of online audience that uses social networks like Facebook, continue to be the most engaged. Facebook reported that visitors who sign in with Facebook on The Huffington Post view 22% more pages and spend eight minutes longer there than the average reader.

Those who sign in to NHL.com with Facebook spend 85% more time and read 90% more articles than the average user. The stats go on and on from major companies to small businesses: they are finding that the social network-engaged Internet user most often becomes their most loyal and valuable customer. As more and more companies and major media sites entrench social plugins into the technology we use, the use and reach of such social media channels will continue to expand.

an integrated like button
= 300% increase
in referral traffic

Figure 8.3: The traffic impact of a Facebook like button.

More Connected Buildings and Spaces In the Future

We are already seeing the Internet enter home technologies outside of the computer screen. Depending on your cable television provider, you may already have the capability of recording your favorite television show on your home digital video recorder while away from home via your office computer or your smartphone. In fact, some cable television providers even allow you to access Facebook and YouTube through your digital television so you can chat with friends or leave comments on a television show's social page or forum while you watch your favorite programs.

And for people who want to have more control of their home while they are away, they can opt for installing smart home technology which allows them to virtually interact with anything that is electronic in the home beyond just the television. Imagine having your favorite song playing when you walk in the door or the lights in your house automatically dimming when you turn on a movie. The costs associated with installing such systems start at around $10,000 while Bill Gates' customized version was estimated to cost $100 million. The possibilities of connecting the physical world to the virtual are just beginning.

Social media technology is all around us and will continue to be more and more woven into our everyday routines even when we are away from the computer. In 2011, New York City Mayor Michael Bloomberg announced that the city now provides free Wi-Fi in all its parks: http://www.nyc.gov/portal/site/nycgov/menu-item.c0935b9a57bb4ef3daf2f1c701c789a0/index.jsp?pageID=mayor_press_release&catID=1194&doc_name=http%3A%2F%2Fwww.nyc.gov%2Fhtml%2Fom%2Fhtml%2F2011a%2Fpr202-11.html&cc=unused1978&rc=1194&ndi=1).

As digital content becomes more easily accessed in public spaces — whether through a Wi-Fi connected laptop, tablet, your mobile phone or Google's Project Glass, the wearable computer in a streamlined glasses frame (slated for release in 2014), customers are increasingly consuming and creating content 24-7. Social media is the latest evolution in how we communicate. Your customers, even those who aren't on Facebook or Twitter, are using the content on the social web to make their purchasing decisions.

Get started with the freeware and cheapware social media tools readily available today and use them to share ideas, learn, and market yourself, your company and its thought leaders. Technology is evolving quickly to meet the way that we live, work and play. If we don't apply ourselves in learning and using the tools we have today, we won't be open to social, political and organizational innovations that occur tomorrow.

9
GLOSSARY

Analytics

Website analytics is the collection, presentation and analysis of information about site users' behavior for the purposes of reporting, learning from and optimizing a website for an improved user experience.

App

App is smart phone slang (initiated by the iPhone) for an application that performs a specific function on your personal device or computer.

Blog

The term "blog" comes from "web log". A blog is an online journal that is interactive and allows visitors to leave comments. Blogs often provide commentary or news on a particular subject, although some function as personal online diaries. Bloggers can add new text, images and videos to their blogs without having to know any web programming, which is the primary reason for the rapid growth in popularity of blogging among all types of Internet users.

Blogger

A blogger is the title given to the person writing blog entries.

Blogging

Blogging is a term used to describe the act of writing a blog.

Click-Throughs

A click-through is a type of digital metric that refers to the act of literally clicking on a link and going to a web page. When talking about click-throughs in online advertising, The click-through rate (CTR) is a metric for measuring success. The CTR for an online ad is defined as the number of clicks on an advertisement divided by the number of times the ad is shown.

Crowdsourcing

Crowdsourcing refers to an open call for input or contributions on specified subject, product or solution to perform business-related tasks that would otherwise have been done by the company itself. Social media simplifies crowdsourcing by providing access to a larger pool of potential respondents.

Digital Metrics

Digital metrics refers to marketing activity and actions you can measure online, such as traffic to your web site, click-throughs from a banner ad or opens from an email message. Digital metrics can be tracked through a variety of web analytics programs.

Direct Message

In Twitter you can send a private 140-character message, called a direct message, to anyone who follows you, but you can only receive messages from people whom you also follow.

Embedding

Embedding is the act of inserting a line of code into web content for the purpose of sharing a video, photo or image that is hosted somewhere else.

Facebook Friends

Facebook friend is a term that describes the people in your personal Facebook network. Facebook friends are those people you have approved and granted access to view your Facebook updates. Facebook friends are able to view and comment on each other's Facebook pages.

Facebook Plugin

A Facebook plugin is an embeddable social feature that can be integrated in your website with a line of HTML. Because the social plugin is hosted by Facebook, it is personalized for all users who are currently logged into Facebook, even if they are visiting your site for the first time.

Feed

See RSS Feed

Guest Blogging

Guest blogging is the act of contributing one or more blog posts to blog owned and managed by a third party.

Hashtags

Twitter hashtags were developed as a way to create topic groups on Twitter. Using hashtags provides an easy way to locate and keep track of conversations on specific topics of interest. Twitter hashtags begin with # and are followed by a keyword phrase such as #design or #build.

Keywords

Keywords is a term used when someone enters specific words or phrases into a search field on a website describing more information they hope to find. Keywords are also used by search engines in order to find, categorize and rank web pages so they can display the best option for internet users looking for related information.

Keyword–friendly

Keyword-friendly is a term used by search engine optimization professionals when describing a web page, post or comment online that was written for the search engines. In other words, specific keyword phrases were added to the page or post in hopes that the search engines will find and rank it.

Klout Score

A Klout score is one way to measure a person's online influence. The score ranges from 1 -100 and is based on calculating variables from different social channels including Faceook and Twitter. Developed by a San Francisco, California-based company called Klout, the Klout score measures the size of a person's online audience, likelihood that a person's message will get amplified or shared online, and overall influence of that person's engaged audience.

Like

Like is a term used by Facebook to show support of a website, product, photo, comment or other type of online information. For a user to like something online, they must be either on Facebook or viewing a website that uses the Facebook like plugin while logged into their Facebook account. The online content the user liked will then show up in their Facebook profile.

Lists

In Twitter you can organize the accounts you follow by categorizing them in lists. Lists can be made public or kept private. Others can subscribe to or follow your public lists that interest them.

Modified Tweet

Similar to a retweet (RT). Indicate your tweet is a modified tweet (MT) when you are significantly altering the original tweet, by using MT instead of RT. (*see Retweet.*)

Pay-Per-Click

A pay-per-click campaign is a type of online ad buy where the advertiser only pays when a web user clicks on their advertisement. The most common pay-per-click campaigns are offered by search engines such as MSN, Yahoo! or Google AdWords. In a search engine pay-per-click campaign, an advertiser can bid on keywords that they want their ad and website link to be found under. Advertisers can bid anywhere from $0.05 to upwards of $10+ per click. They are only charged when a user clicks on the ad and visits their web site.

Posting

Posting refers to the act of adding content including a comment, photo or other information to a website or social network.

Retweet

Retweet is a term used to describe the act of re-posting some else's tweet to your own Twitter feed. Having your tweet retweeted is desirable because it helps your tweet gain exposure on other people's Twitter accounts and reach more people online. The format is "RT @ username" where username is the twitter handle of the person you are retweeting.

RSS Feeds

RSS feeds (or really simple syndication) is a type of web feed format used to easily and automatically publish frequently updated information such as news headlines and blog updates. RSS feeds are read by using software called an RSS reader or aggregator, which can be website or desktop based or work on various mobile devices.

Search Engines

A search engine is an online tool that allows a user to search for information on the World Wide Web through a variety of keyword phrases. Google and Bing are two examples of search engines.

Search Engine Optimization

Search engine optimization is the process of organizing a website and its content to improve the chance that it will be included near the top of search engine rankings by considering search engines' criteria for gathering, evaluating and ranking information.

Share

A share in social media refers to any way a user chooses to pass content along to their online social networks. Many blogs and websites have social plugins that make sharing easy by providing immediate access to the user's Twitter, Facebook or other social media profiles for the purpose of sharing the link.

Smart Phone

A smart phone is a hand-held device that offers more functionality beyond standard mobile phone services. Common features include email, web access, and the ability to add apps that perform a specific function.

Social Bookmarking

Social bookmarking is a way for internet users to note, organize and store favorite websites, pages and online resources on a platform that can be located anywhere.

Spam

Spam refers to unsolicited bulk email, junk mail or posts,. Commercial email that a recipient has not requested or "opted in" for is considered spam.

Tag

A tag is a keyword added to a blog post, image, photo or video for the purposes of helping visitors find content that is related to their interests.

Tag Cloud

A tag cloud is a visual representation of the most commonly used or most popular tags on a particular site.

Thought Leader

A thought leader refers to someone who has influential and innovative ideas related to a specific industry that merit attention and discussion.

Troll

A troll refers to a person who is overly critical and posts hurtful, damaging and/or negative comments anonymously on the social web.

Tweets

A tweet is the term used for a post that is made on Twitter.

Tweet Chat

A tweet chat is a pre arranged, topic-focused gathering on Twitter. Tweet chat's often have a leader or moderator and sometimes a predetermined agenda. Participants contribute to and follow the discussion through tweets that include a pre-established hashtag (like #AECSM, which takes place Tuesdays at 1pm PST).

Tweetup

A tweetup is an organized or impromptu in-person gathering of people who interact on Twitter.

Twitter Followers

A Twitter follower is someone who has opted to receive the tweets posted by another Twitter user.

Webcasting

The action of using the web to deliver live or previously recorded broadcasts.

Webinar

A webinar is an online seminar with presentation materials available through an online interface. Typically, attendees register in advance, log in at the specified time for access to live audio and presentation

materials. Most webinars include a Q&A feature that allows participants to pose questions during or at the end of the presentations.

Widgets

A web widget is a small application that can be installed on a web page,
often with a few lines of code. They are typically created in DHTML,
JavaScript or Adobe Flash. Online tools such as date/time clocks,
stock market tickers and daily weather are all examples of widgets.

Wi-Fi

Wi-Fi refers to a wireless internet connection or wireless networking
standards.

ABOUT THE AUTHORS

Holly Berkley

Holly Berkley is a recognized Internet Marketing expert who has developed web sites, online marketing strategies and corporate social media training programs for some of today's top companies. She developed the first Interactive Marketing and Social Media Marketing courses for San Diego State University where she continues to teach as a guest lecturer. She is also the author of the popular business books *"Marketing in the New Media"* and *"Low Budget Online Marketing for Small Business"* which are also published by Self Counsel Press.

Holly Berkley lives in San Diego, California where she continues to work as an independent Internet Marketing Consultant.

hollyb@berkweb.com

www.berkweb.com

Amanda Walter

Amanda Walter is a "behind the scenes" PR professional who has worked inside some of the biggest brands in A/E and directly with some of the top executives and individuals whose ideas are shaping today's industry landscape. In 2010, she founded Walter Communications where she continues to help designers and planners of the built environment communicate their ideas, projects and firms through print, online and social media, as well as through public speaking.

Amanda specializes in developing broad communications programs with her clients for their advocacy, thought leadership and social media initiatives. She lives in the San Francisco Bay Area with her husband and two kids. Connect with and learn more about Amanda at www.waltercomms.com.

amanda@waltercomms.com

www.waltercomms.com